DISCOVERING
KING ARTHUR

DISCOVERING
KING ARTHUR

Beryl Beare

quantum

LONDON • NEW YORK • TORONTO • SYDNEY

quantum

An imprint of W. Foulsham & Co. Ltd
The Publishing House, Bennetts Close,
Cippenham, Slough, Berkshire, SL1 5AP, England

For my husband, John, who first introduced me to Arthur –
and then let us form our own relationship.

'And for to pass the time this book shall be pleasant to read in,
but for to give faith and belief that all is true and that is
contained herein, ye be at your liberty.'
From Caxton's Prologue to *Morte D'Arthur*

ISBN 0-572-02367-7
Copyright © 1999 Beryl Davies

Photographs courtesy of Mary Evans Picture Library

Typeset in Great Britain by Grafica, Bournemouth
Printed in Great Britain by St Edmundsbury Press, Bury St Edmunds, Suffolk

Contents

Foreword
By Geoffrey Ashe

o entitle a book *Discovering King Arthur* is to invite a query. Who exactly is going to be discovered? A reader might suspect, with an excusable sinking of the heart, that this is another search for the 'historical' Arthur. There have been too many of these, too many theories, with a marked tendency to refute each other. Beryl Beare has no such intention. She accepts that there is a real person lurking somewhere, but without trying to discuss or identify him. It isn't going to be that sort of discovery.

My own interest in the Arthurian legend is perhaps worth tracing because, while it followed another course, I can see a kind of convergence. The first phase was a definite non-interest. True, I must have known something at the age of nine or ten. I was a devotee of Richmal Crompton's 'William' stories. In one of them William and his friends formed themselves into the Knights of the Square Table and undertook to right wrongs. I recall that this didn't have to be explained to me. The reason may have been that somebody had given me a book of legends for children which included Arthurian ones. I have a memory of that too. I liked the Greek and the Norse, but not the Arthurian. There, my only abiding image is a colour plate reproducing a picture of Galahad kneeling before the Grail, which hung in the air looking like an athletics trophy surrounded by light. It impressed me not at all.

Involvement came eventually, not at first with Arthur, but with Glastonbury. I was drawn in by that place's haunting mélange of sanctity, history and mythology. When I began writing a book about it, I soon grasped how vital a part the Arthurian legend played. The Grail was brought there, the King himself was reputedly buried there. All this had to be looked into. Looking into it, I realised – and was to realise increasingly through further research and other projects – that Arthur was more interesting than I had thought. The tradition was many-layered and many-faceted.

I believed, and believe still, that there is a real person at the starting point. Yet when you have said that, you haven't said much. Arthur proliferates. Different generations of storytellers find different things in him, or impose different concepts on him. He can be a Celtic war leader, a ruler of fairyland, a sort of emperor, a medieval monarch accompanied by knights in armour and beautiful ladies. He can be a demigod or an allegory. In folklore, he can be a giant. Over the centuries his legend keeps fading out and returning. It returns changed. One or two ideas of him are recurrent. Thus, he is usually the focus of a long-ago golden age. But that age is dreamed of variously, according to the imaginings of the dreamer.

The phenomenon is not single or even consistent. It is richly multiple, with a shape-shifting hero. When I did come to take an interest in the romantic Arthur, it was mainly because I had learned to see him in depth, as a medieval embodiment of a myth quite differently embodied at other times.

Beryl Beare's selection has the special merit of revealing some of the multiplicity. Many people have read, as children, one of the countless junior Arthur books (probably based on Malory, expurgated) and grown up assuming that this is the whole story. It isn't, and Beryl shows that it isn't. Boldly, she retells the anonymous Welsh tale *Culhwch and Olwen*. With its formidable names, its barbaric adventures, its fantastic characters and weird monsters, it is conspicuously unlike anything else. To a reader accustomed to the romantic Arthur, it comes as a shock. Is this the real thing at all?

Well, I knew a teacher of children of nine or ten, who got hold of a simplified version of it and read it to the class. They enjoyed it. So, she thought, she had an Arthurian opening. She tried introducing them to the Round Table and other medieval matters. That didn't interest them any more than it interested me at the same age. For these children, Arthur meant *Culhwch and Olwen!*

As for the known authors whom Beryl so skilfully adapts, I am pleased to find Geoffrey of Monmouth given a good innings. Writing in Latin in the 1130s, he is the transitional genius between the world of older tradition and the world of romance. His inventive *History of the Kings of Britain* is one of the key books of the Middle Ages. It contains a great deal besides Arthur. Shakespeare's Lear, for instance, makes his début in it. Geoffrey's narrative of Arthur himself, in post-Roman Britain, becomes virtually the King's official biography. It has too much about wars and conquests, even extending into Gaul (now France), but it launches Guinevere and other leading characters, tells of the founding of Arthur's order of knighthood, and gives a lavish description of his court that prepares the way for the imagery of Camelot. Here is one version of the Arthurian golden age.

Geoffrey is not a historian, and can never be relied on for facts. But in most of his book he does make use of history – or what he would like to think is history – to create his fiction. Sometimes we can see where it comes from. His account of Vortigern and Merlin, Beryl's first act, and part of his account of Arthur, derive from a text by a ninth-century Welsh monk. That takes us a certain distance, but not very far. However, he tries to convince his readers that the *History of the Kings of Britain* has a broader and firmer basis than they might suppose. He claims to have translated it from 'a certain very ancient book written in the British language', meaning Welsh or possibly Breton. This book has never been found, and the statement is incredible as it stands. Still, in recent years Geoffrey has gained a little ground against his detractors. In the episodes of warfare in Gaul, there is reason to think he has taken hints from an authentic record of a 'King of the Britons', who may even have been the original Arthur. But this is not a topic to embark upon here.

Geoffrey supplied the framework for the Arthurian romances that followed. Most of the countries of western and central

Europe contributed. For more than a hundred years, Arthur's Britain was the favourite setting for imaginative fiction. The warfare receded somewhat, giving place to chivalry, courtly love, knightly adventures, tournaments, quests. New themes entered – the Round Table, Camelot, the Grail. For a time, French authors dominated the field. At length the continental nations lost interest. Sir Thomas Malory, in the fifteenth century, is a late arrival, translating and adapting previous romances and often improving them. He establishes a kind of orthodoxy for the whole cycle that endures into modern times.

He has his own ideas of the golden age. The King is still a war leader as with Geoffrey, and his chief foreign campaign is actually more successful. But Malory puts it much earlier in the reign than Geoffrey does, making room for a long peace to ensue. Arthur's Britain is a chivalric Utopia. The knights are frequently violent, and Malory doesn't pretend that they entirely lived up to their ideals, but he is clear that the ideals were affirmed. While most of the time he is frankly storytelling, he has a serious intent that occasionally shows through. He is critical of his own contemporaries, and implies a contrast between Arthur's regime and the reality of England during the Wars of the Roses, with rival kings fighting each other and rival lords betraying each other.

He also draws a contrast of a non-political kind. Speaking of love between men and women, he says that in Arthur's time it was marked by truth and faithfulness … and patience. A couple could live tranquilly for years without being in a hurry to have sexual relations. 'But nowadays,' says Malory, 'men cannot love seven night but they must have all their desires: that love may not endure by reason; for where they be soon accorded and hasty, heat soon it cooleth. Right so fareth love nowadays, soon hot soon cold: there is no stability.' This is the fifteenth century speaking, not the twentieth! It should be remarked, however, that when Malory praises the love of olden times, he doesn't say anything about marriage. Passing to the next author, we find a changed atmosphere.

Tennyson is altogether more complex. One impulse behind his *Idylls of the King* was a personal tragedy, the death of an adored friend, Arthur Hallam. His long poem *In Memoriam* traces his reflections on death and immortality, leading him slowly from despair to a belief that in some inscrutable sense, Hallam still lives. Before *In Memoriam* he had written poems on Arthurian themes, but his experience drew him more powerfully towards Hallam's namesake, the King, apparently dead, who was still living in some secret Avalon and would return. In *Merlin and the Gleam* the poet overlaps the enchanter and the two Arthurs coalesce.

Other motives at work in the *Idylls of the King* were Tennyson's appointment as Poet Laureate and his admiration for Prince Albert, Victoria's husband. As the series took shape in the hands of the Crown's poet, Arthur came to resemble the Prince Consort. After Albert's untimely death Tennyson dedicated the *Idylls of the King* to his memory. He met the Queen and she drew parallels between her own loss and his. His attitude to her became romantic and chivalrous, and he warmly upheld the values she stood for.

The main structure of the *Idylls of the King* is taken from Malory, but Tennyson invents a good deal himself, and the moral shift is profound. He treats the Arthurian legend as allegorical, shadowing 'Sense at war with Soul', the conflict between the baser and the higher in human nature. Arthur tries to create a spiritually inspired monarchy. The Round Table stands for ideals of courage, honour, and so forth, as ever – but also sexual correctness. Here Victorian values take charge. Holy matrimony enters the story. It symbolises the spirit's mastery of the unruly flesh. Many of the knights have wives, and the amours of medieval romance, when mentioned at all, are firmly condemned.

As a result, Guinevere suffers. Her illicit love for Lancelot is now crucial and functional. Tennyson makes it the fatal flaw at the heart of the regime. The Queen's example breeds cynicism and moral decline. There is also a doubt about Arthur's origin and his right to reign. In the end, evil elements exploit this and overthrow the good. What remains is an impression that while spiritually inspired monarchy has failed, it was worth trying, it embodies an aspiration that must not perish. This imposition of

Victorian standards gets Tennyson into difficulties. It makes an adultery central to the plot, yet prevents him from giving an account of it. Such explicitness would be improper. Arthur's downfall results from a love affair so important that it should have an episode to itself, but it can be handled only by allusions and flashbacks.

Tennyson's public didn't mind. His writings were genuinely popular. He was a best seller as poets seldom are. For that reason, the *Idylls of the King* had an influence outside literature. Most of them appeared during a time when republicanism was a serious political force, owing to the Queen's reclusive neglect of duty. Tennyson would have none of this. He gave his Arthurian cycle an epilogue loyally addressed to her. The tide turned, and while of course much greater factors were at work, the Laureate's presentation of mystical monarchy undoubtedly helped the Crown to regain its glamour.

None of the foregoing discussion presumes to be a commentary on Beryl Beare's work, which stands up convincingly on its own. These are supplementary notes, no more. Still, I am pleased and honoured to have the privilege of contributing.

Introduction

his is not intended as an academic book but, essentially, as a voyage of discovery. I hope that it will also prove to be a good read, for it was when I discovered the drama and sheer delight of the stories in the Arthurian legend that I realised the form I wanted the book to take.

The Arthurian stories have been told and retold of course, but never, I believe, in this way. I have selected stories from the most important and best known of the British authors: Geoffrey of Monmouth, Malory, *The Mabinogion* and Tennyson, in that order (the final tale, The Death of Arthur, is also from Malory), because they are representative of the best of the Arthurian cycle, although they by no means include it all, and I have arranged them more or less consecutively. Malory outweighs the other authors and I make no apology for this; any 'discovering' of King Arthur must necessarily give precedence to the very fountainhead of English Arthurian fiction.

Because the stories have been chosen for their dramatic impact, they are divided into acts, and scenes within acts, but they are told in straightforward narrative form. I have tried to maintain the feeling and mood of the original, and have introduced each act and scene with a brief passage from the source, presented in drama format.

I was particularly apprehensive about the Tennyson, feeling it was audacious, and perhaps rash, to attempt to reduce the beauty of his heightened language into narrative prose; 'Gareth and Lynette', however, seemed to work well as a narrative tale, so I hope that perhaps Tennyson might forgive me!

I have included the sort of information I should have been grateful to find in one single volume during my own research: a brief description of the characters (The Players – in which I have included Morgan le Fay and the questing beast because of their importance in the legends, although they only appear briefly in these stories) some simple information about the geographical and political situation in fifth and sixth-century Britain (Setting the Scene); a brief synopsis of the Arthurian story (Prologue) and finally some information about the authors and their sources and the influence of Arthur on our culture today (Viewed from the Wings).

As the legend is derived from so many sources, and translations of sources, it is inevitable that the spelling of the names of persons and places varies considerably in the Arthurian cycle. I have tended to use the spelling of the original source author unless I have felt it to be too confusing or obscure, in which case I have used a modern or more common spelling. In order to maintain narrative flow in the stories, I have used parentheses, rather than footnotes or separate notes, where a word or phrase seems to need explanation.

I have made no attempt to try to establish the true identity – or indeed existence – of King Arthur, but leave that to those with much more knowledge. Suffice it to say that there was a historic ruler, or chieftain, living in Britain in the fifth or sixth century; whether he was the Arthur of legend or not is a moot point. Personally, I don't think it matters. After all, Falstaff is every bit as real to us as Prince Hal, perhaps even more so, and if Arthur *is* enigmatic it certainly doesn't detract from his popularity. Long may the legend reign.

Notes on the Pronunciation of Welsh Names

It is unlikely that anyone but a Welsh speaker will be able to pronounce the names correctly; in fact since the spellings vary, it is doubtful that we have a definitive pronunciation anyway. However, I hope these notes will prove helpful. This is taken from *The Romance of Arthur* (ed. James J. Wilhelm).

a as in father

ai, au, and ei as in aisle

aw as in now

c as in cat

ch as in Scottish loch

dd as in then

e as in bed

f as in of

ff as in effect

g as in go

i as in bid

th as in think

u as in busy or bead

w as in with or as the vowels in tooth

y as in myth or city in a single or final syllable and as alive or glove in other syllables

Pronounce ll with the tongue in the same position as for l by gently blowing air, without voice, past the side of the tongue (the l in English clean is very similar).

In Welsh, the stressed syllable is almost always the next-to-last syllable.

The Players

These are the main characters in the stories, in order of appearance. Beneath each player are the names of the original authors in whose stories they appear.

Vortigern

Geoffrey of Monmouth
Usurper king who joined forces with the Saxon leaders Hengist and Horsa, and then fled to Wales to build himself a tower on Dinas Emrys, the foundations of which repeatedly sank into the earth. Merlin attributed this to the actions of two dragons in a subterranean lake, which later proved to be true.

Merlin

Geoffrey of Monmouth, Malory, Tennyson
Magician and prophet who became Arthur's counsellor. He was thought to be the offspring of an incubus (evil spirit) and a human mother. He made many prophecies, including the discovery of the dragons beneath Vortigern's tower, and brought the 'Giants' Dance' – Stonehenge – from Ireland. He took Arthur from King Uther at birth and gave him into the care of Sir Ector. He finally succumbed to the charms of Nimue, a maiden of the lake, revealing to her the secrets of his magic, which she then used to imprison him in a cave.

Aurelius Ambrosius

Geoffrey of Monmouth
Brother to Uther and King Constans. He slew Vortigern in revenge for Constans' death and defeated the Saxons.

Uther Pendragon

Geoffrey of Monmouth, Malory
Succeeded Aurelius as king and fathered Arthur by Igraine of Cornwall.

Arthur

Malory, Mabinigion, Tennyson
The son of Uther Pendragon and Igraine, and adopted at birth
by Sir Ector, he became king of all England and defeated the
Saxons in many battles. He established the Knights of the
Round Table at his court at Camelot, married Guinevere and
later ordered her to be burnt for her alleged infidelity with
Sir Lancelot. He was eventually killed by Mordred, his own son
by his half-sister, Margawse (daughter of Igraine).

Morgan le Fay

Malory
Youngest daughter of Igraine, well versed in the magic arts, she
tried to kill Arthur (her half-brother) by magic on several
occasions. She showed compassion when he was fatally
wounded, however, and took him to Avalon.

Lot

Malory, Tennyson
The king of Orkney and Norway who married Margawse, half-
sister to Arthur. Gawain, Gaheris and Gareth were his sons.

Margawse

Malory, Bellicent in Tennyson
Wife of King Lot and half-sister to Arthur, by whom she bore
Mordred.

Mordred

Malory, Tennyson
Arthur's son and also his nephew – being the product of
Arthur's incestuous union with his half-sister, Margawse. Left as
regent while Arthur was at war with Lancelot, Mordred faked
news of Arthur's death and had himself elected king. He tried to
marry Guinevere, but she barricaded herself in the Tower of
London. Mordred was slain at Camlann, where he fatally
wounded Arthur.

Guinevere

Malory
The daughter of King Leodegrance, Arthur married her against Merlin's advice. She was suspected of having a love affair with Lancelot, who saved her from being burnt.

Questing Beast

Malory
A strange beast (said to have the head of a snake, body of a leopard, hindquarters of a lion and feet of a hart) from whose stomach issued the sound of baying hounds. Hunted by King Pellinore, but never brought to earth.

Lady of the Lake

Malory, Tennyson
The mysterious lady who gave Arthur the sword, Excalibur. Sometimes identified with Nimue, a maiden of the lake.

Balin

Malory
The knight with the two swords who slew the Lady of the Lake and struck King Pellam with the dolorous (grievous) blow that laid waste to three countries.

Balan

Malory
Brother to Balin; each unknowingly slew the other. They were buried together.

Gawain

Tennyson, Malory
One of Arthur's most prominent knights and his nephew, the
eldest son of Lot and Margawse. He declared war on Lancelot for
the death of his brothers, Gaheris and Gareth, and was finally
killed fighting for Arthur against Mordred.

Culhwch

Mabinogion
Son of King Cilydd. He sought Olwen, the beautiful daughter of
Ysbaddaden Chief Giant, for his bride and was given numerous
tasks by the giant before he could win her – most of which
Arthur accomplished for him.

Olwen

Mabinogion
Daughter of Ysbaddaden Chief Giant, beloved of Culhwch.

Bedivere

Bedwyr in Mabinogion, *Malory*
An important Knight of the Round Table and companion to
Arthur. One of only two survivors – with his brother, Lucan the
Butler – of the terrible final battle with Mordred. He was
charged with returning Arthur's sword, Excalibur, to the Lady of
the Lake.

Gareth

Tennyson, Malory
Youngest son of King Lot and Margawse (Bellicent). He joined
Arthur's court as a kitchen boy, was knighted by Arthur and
accidentally killed in battle by Lancelot.

Lancelot

Tennyson, Malory

The most famous of Arthur's knights and the king's champion.
He fell in love with Guinevere and, in doing battle to defend
both her honour and his own, accidentally killed the knight he
loved most, Gareth (and then also Gareth's brother, Gaheris).
Arthur and Gareth's brother, Gawain, declared war against him.
Gawain, on his deathbed, wrote a letter of reconciliation to him
but Lancelot did not arrive in England in time to assist Arthur in
his fatal last battle with Mordred.

Lynette

Tennyson

The damsel for whom Gareth undertook the quest of defeating
the three knights of the stream and the knight who called
himself Death.

Setting the Scene

In about AD 400 Britain was a province of the Roman Empire. Many people in the south lived in Roman towns or in country houses with central heating and mosaic floors. But when the Roman army left Britain in 406, living standards rapidly deteriorated for the Celts and Britons left behind.

Picts from the north and Scots from Ireland attacked northern England, and sometime between 440 and 460, Germanic Saxons invaded the country from across the North Sea. Some sources say that King Vortigern invited the Saxon leaders to Britain to help him fight the Picts and Scots.

Invited or not, the Saxons arrived in hordes and, over the course of the next four centuries, set about claiming the land. They were barbarians with neither armour nor cavalry, but despite their lack of military equipment, they seem to have been effective conquerors, for the Britons only succeeded in holding Cornwall, Wales and Strathclyde against them.
With the Saxons and Jutes came the Angles (hence 'Anglo-Saxons'), a Germanic tribe originating from the Angelm district of Schleswig in southern Denmark. They settled in Northumbria, Mercia and East Anglia and England is named after them. The Arthurian stories tell us that King Arthur held off these Anglo-Saxon raiders in the fifth or sixth century, and that he fought twelve battles against them; the final, decisive battle being the seige of Mount Badon, in which the Britons were victorious.

Archaeological excavations give us some indication of the Saxon way of life. Most villages consisted of three or four farms, with buildings of wood and thatch. Teams of up to eight oxen were used to work the land, and dogs were kept to drive the sheep and guard against wolves. Crops of oats, wheat, rye and barley were grown and, in addition to meat, fish such as perch and pike were probably eaten.

Britain in the Early Sixth Century

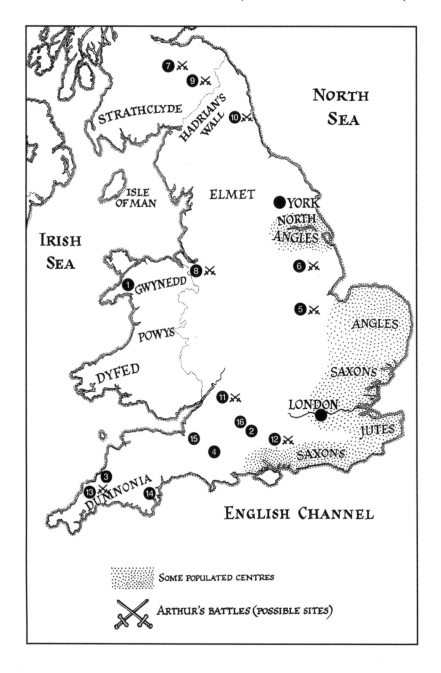

NORTH SEA

STRATHCLYDE

HADRIAN'S WALL

ISLE OF MAN

ELMET

YORK

NORTH ANGLES

IRISH SEA

GWYNEDD

POWYS

DYFED

ANGLES

SAXONS

LONDON

JUTES

SAXONS

DUMNONIA

ENGLISH CHANNEL

SOME POPULATED CENTRES

ARTHUR'S BATTLES (POSSIBLE SITES)

Map Key and Place Names

The possible sites given for King Arthur's twelve battles against the Saxons (map references 5–11) are mentioned in the *Welsh History of the Britons,* a mixture of history and legend written in the ninth century by Nennius.

1. **Dinas Emrys** A wooded hill near Beddgelert in Gwynedd, Wales. Here Vortigern attempted to build his tower and was advised to sacrifice a fatherless child – Merlin. (Geoffrey of Monmouth)

2. **Stonehenge** The 'Giants' Ring' on Salisbury Plain, England. The stones were brought from Ireland and erected by Merlin. (Geoffrey of Monmouth)

3. **Tintagel** On the northern coast of Cornwall, the site of a castle belonging to Duke Gorlois, where a union between Gorlois' wife and Uther Pendragon resulted in the birth of Arthur. (Malory)

4. **Cadbury Castle** In Somerset, between Yeovil and Wincanton, the site most popularly believed to be that of Camelot, where King Arthur resided and held his court.

5. **'Glein'** At the mouth of this river Arthur led his first battle against the Saxons.

6. **'Linnuis'** In this region, on the banks of another river, Arthur fought the next four battles against the Saxons.

   'Bassas' The unidentified site of Arthur's sixth battle.

7. **'Celidon'** Here, in a wood known as 'Coit Celidon', Arthur fought his seventh battle against the Saxons.

   'Castle Guinnion' Another unidentified site; the scene of Arthur's eighth battle, during which he carried a statue of the Virgin Mary on his shoulders and was victorious.

8. **Chester** 'City of the Legions', the site of Arthur's ninth battle against the Saxons.

9. **'Tribruit'** Arthur's tenth battle was on the banks of this river.

10. **Rochester** Arthur's eleventh battle was in this area, on the hill of 'Agned', possibly located at High Rochester in Northumberland.

11. **Bath** 'Mount Badon', the site of Arthur's twelfth and final battle against the Saxons, in which he totally defeated them. Several other sites have been suggested for Badon, including Badbury Hill and Liddington Castle, near Swindon in Wiltshire, England.

12. **Winchester** Said to be Arthur's capital and the site of Camelot (Malory). Here, Arthur fought his second battle against the usurping Mordred, defeating him and finally pursuing him to Camlann. The huge round table top in Castle Hall was thought, for many years, to be Arthur's original Round Table – in fact it dates from the fourteenth century.

13. **Camelford** North Cornwall, one of several sites suggested for Camlann, scene of Arthur's final battle against Mordred, in which Mordred died and Arthur was mortally wounded.

14. **Dozmary Pool** On Bodmin Moor, the traditional Cornish location for the Camlann battle. It may also be the water into which Sir Bedivere cast the sword Excalibur, although various other lakes have also been suggested as sites for this episode.

15. **Glastonbury** Reputedly Avalon, the 'Fortunate Island' to which Arthur was taken after being mortally wounded. In 1190 or early 1191, a grave was discovered here with a coffin in it containing what were said to be the bones of Arthur and Guinevere. These were subsequently placed in a marble tomb in the Abbey Church. The site of the exhumation was apparently forgotten, but was rediscovered in 1962–63.

16. **Amesbury** North of Salisbury. Queen Guinevere came to Amesbury Abbey on hearing of Arthur's death. (Malory)

Prologue

(The story according to Malory)

Arthur was the son of King Uther Pendragon and Igraine, wife of the Duke of Cornwall, whom Uther won with the help of Merlin's magic. In repayment for his help, Merlin demanded that any child of the union be delivered to him at birth. This condition was duly met. Merlin handed the boy into the safe-keeping of the good Sir Ector with the result that Arthur grew up unaware of his royal parentage.

At the age of 15, Arthur succeeded where all others had failed. He drew a magic sword from a stone and so proved himself to be the true-born king of England. Once crowned, and having overcome those nobles who rebelled against him, Arthur led an army against the Saxons and defeated them at Lincoln, Celidon Wood and Bath. He then raised the siege of York and restored the city to its former glory, reinstating Lot and two other dispossessed Yorkist princes.

Infatuated with Lot's wife, Margawse, Arthur slept with her – not realising that she was one of Igraine's daughters and therefore his own half-sister. The result of this incestuous union was the boy Mordred, destined to bring about Arthur's downfall. Arthur then fell in love with Guinevere, a lady of noble Roman birth who was reputed to be the most beautiful woman in Britain. Merlin, who had become the king's mentor, warned him that the marriage would bring sorrow, but Arthur was too much in love to heed his magician on this occasion, and married Guinevere anyway.

Despite his reservations, Merlin agreed to deliver a wedding gift to the king from Guinevere's father – a magnificent round table at which all Arthur's knights could be seated without dispute as to places of honour. One of the places was left unoccupied, however; the Seige (or seat) Perilous was reserved for the holiest of knights who would, alone, succeed in the Quest for the Holy Grail. This knight proved to be Sir Galahad, the son of Sir Lancelot, whose birth was the result of a night of passion between Lancelot and King Pelles' daughter, Elaine. It was a liaison into which Lancelot had been tricked by an enchantment of Arthur's sister, Morgan le Fay.

King Arthur held his court at Camelot, and soon the fame of his noble Knights of the Round Table spread throughout the world. With the aid of his sword, Excalibur – presented to him by the Lady of the Lake – he had led his army to victory in battle and had himself defeated many enemies. Now that he had reunited the entire kingdom there was time for questing and adventure, chivalry and tournaments, for the slaying of beasts, giants and dragons – and the punishing of knights who dishonoured ladies.

Among his own knights, Arthur had great affection for Sir Kay, his foster-brother, and Sir Bedivere, but dearest to his heart was the brave Sir Lancelot. Therefore when he was told of an affair between Lancelot and Guinevere, he refused to believe it. If true, it meant that Merlin's prophecy had been correct. But now the magician was no longer there to advise him, for Merlin had lost his magic to Nimue, a lady of the lake, and she had imprisoned him for all time.

However, Mordred, with his brother Agravain and twelve other knights, succeeded in trapping Sir Lancelot in the queen's bed-chamber, and Arthur was forced to accept the truth. Guinevere was sentenced to be burnt at the stake, but Lancelot rescued her and carried her off to his castle, Joyous Gard.

Reluctantly, Arthur waged war on Lancelot, leaving Sir Mordred as regent in his absence. Mordred was quick to seize his opportunity, forging reports of the king's death and taking the crown for himself. On hearing of this, Arthur returned to do battle with his son, defeating him twice before following him to Camlann, where Mordred was killed and the king was mortally wounded.

Arthur told Sir Bedivere to take his enchanted sword, Excalibur, and cast it into a nearby lake. Distressed at the thought of destroying such a magnificent weapon, Bedivere twice disobeyed the king's order. When, eventually, he did hurl the sword out over the lake, a hand rose from the water and caught it.

King Arthur then instructed Sir Bedivere to take him to the lake and lay him in a waiting barge. The knight did so, and Arthur was borne away to the Isle of Avalon – where some say his wounds were healed, and others say he died and was buried.

ACT ONE

Merlin

From Geoffrey of Monmouth's *History of the Kings of Britain*

VORTIGERN AND MERLIN

THE PROPHECIES OF MERLIN

MERLIN AND THE 'GIANTS' DANCE'
(STONEHENGE)

MERLIN: Wherefore have I and my mother been
called into thy presence?

VORTIGERN: My wizards have declared it unto
me as their counsel ... that I should seek out
one that had never a father, that when I have
sprinkled his blood upon the foundation of my
tower my work should stand firm.

BOOK VI, 19

ortigern, King of Britain, had escaped from his enemies and fled into Wales. Once those same enemies, the Saxons, had been his allies and he had given them anything they asked for. He had even married a pagan woman, the daughter of the Saxon leader Hengist. In exchange for the girl he had given Hengist the whole province of Kent – although, admittedly, the duke who ruled over that territory had been unaware of the transaction.

This had so alarmed the people of Britain that they had forced Vortigern to yield the crown to his son, Vortimer, who sent the Saxons away. After his son's untimely death (poisoned by his pagan step-mother, rumour had it) Vortigern reclaimed the throne and invited the Saxon leaders to return discreetly.

The Saxons, unfortunately, had returned in their thousands, but Hengist sent word to say that he would do whatever King Vortigern wished, and a peaceful meeting was arranged. Peaceful! The treacherous Hengist and his Saxons had betrayed Vortigern's trust and cut the throats of more than four hundred of his barons and earls. Then they marched on London, Lincoln and Winchester, ravaging the country and slaying the people mercilessly as they went.

King Vortigern was no stranger to betrayal and treachery, for he was a usurper. He had gained the throne originally by inciting Pictish soldiers to kill the young King Constans, after which he had taken the crown for himself and had the soldiers beheaded for their 'dastardly crime'. As a consequence of this the Picts had revolted against him, added to which he was afraid of Constans' two brothers, Aureluis Ambrosius and Uther (later to be called Pendragon), who had fled to Brittany in their youth and now, fully grown, were threatening to launch a huge fleet against his kingdom.

When the Saxons first landed in England, it seemed to Vortigern – despite their pagan beliefs – that they must have been God-sent to help him. But now he had seen the worst side of these fearless warriors as they devastated his land, captured his cities and brutally murdered his citizens. They were truly an accursed people and he had no idea what he could do against them.

Escaping with his life (for which he had readily agreed to give anything the Saxons demanded) King Vortigern fled to Wales, summoned his magicians and asked them what he should do. They advised him to build an immensely strong tower where he would be safe, having now lost all his other fortresses. So Vortigern sought a suitable position for his tower, and decided upon Mount Snowdon.

The royal stonemasons were assembled and laid the first foundations, but the following morning all signs of their labour had completely disappeared. And so it continued – no matter how much they built in one day, by the following day the earth had swallowed up every trace of their work.

When Vortigern was told of this he summoned his magicians once more, asking them why such a thing should happen and what could be done to prevent it. In truth the magicians were baffled, but the king required a solution, and a solution he should have. They told him he must seek out a boy who had never had a father, kill him and sprinkle his blood upon the stones and mortar. This, they promised, would make the foundation of the tower hold firm so that the work could progress successfully.

Vortigern immediately dispatched his messengers to look for such a lad. Their task was unenviable; a boy who had never had a father was not easy to find. From the north to the south of Wales they searched diligently, but in vain.

Eventually they came to the city of Carmarthan, where they saw some boys playing a game inside the city gates. Weary with travel, they sat down in a circle to watch the game. It lasted for several hours, ending only when two of the boys suddenly started to quarrel. One of them became very angry.

'You're a fool!' he shouted at the other. 'How can you possibly think you're a match for me? I have royal blood on both sides of my family, and as for you – why, nobody knows who you are, for you never had a father!'

At these words the messengers instantly became alert. They looked keenly at the boy who had been addressed and asked several of the bystanders who he was.

'He is called Merlin,' a man replied. 'No one knows anything of his father, but his mother is the daughter of a king of south Wales and lives with the nuns at St Peter's Church, here in the city.'

The messengers acted at once. They hurried to the governor of the city and ordered him, in the king's name, to send Merlin and his mother to Vortigern. When the governor heard the reason for this command, he immediately sent the boy and his mother to the king.

Vortigern received the mother with courtesy, for he knew she was of royal birth. Then he asked her who had been the father of her child.

'On my very life, my lord – and indeed, on your life too – I never had relations with any man to bear this child,' she replied. 'I know only that when I was with the other nuns in our private chamber, someone used to visit me in the form of a handsome young man. He would hold me tightly and kiss me – then suddenly he would vanish and I could no longer see him. Often, too, if I was sitting alone, he would talk to me without being visible. Having haunted me like this for some time, he then lay with me in the shape of a man and left me with child. This, my lord, I swear to be the truth. You in your wisdom must decide who is the boy's father, for I have told you all I know.'

The king was amazed by what he heard, but felt unsure as to the truth of the story. So he sent for a certain learned man whose knowledge was much respected. The man listened carefully to every detail as the woman repeated the story for his benefit.

The discovery of the infant Arthur from *The Idylls of the King* (Eleanor Fortescue Brickdale) *opposite*

'Is such a thing possible?' the king asked, when she had finished.

'In the books written by our sages, and in many histories as well, I have discovered that quite a number of men have been born in this way,' the learned man replied. He went on to explain.

'Certain spirits are said to live between the moon and the earth. We call them incubus demons. They have partly the nature of men and partly the nature of angels, and when they wish to do so, they can assume human shape and have intercourse with women. It is possible that such a one appeared to this lady and that by him she conceived the boy.'

Merlin, who had been listening to all this, now approached the king.

'Why have my mother and I been called into your presence?' he asked.

'My magicians have told me that I should seek out a boy who never had a father,' Vortigern replied, 'and that when I have sprinkled his blood on the foundation of my tower, the building will stand firm.'

'Call your magicians before me,' said Merlin, 'and I will prove that they lie.'

The king was so amazed by such confident words from one so young that he called the magicians immediately.

'You have no idea what is preventing the foundation of this tower from remaining in place,' Merlin told them scornfully, 'and in your ignorance you advise the king that my blood should be sprinkled on the stones to make the building stand firm. Tell me then, what lies hidden beneath the foundation? There is certainly something that is preventing the tower being built.'

Vivien (Nimue in Malory), a maiden of the lake who stripped Merlin of his magical powers, from *The Idylls of the King* (Eleanor Fortescue Brickdale) *opposite*

The magicians quailed at Merlin's tone, even though he was just a boy. None of them said a word. Merlin then turned to Vortigern. 'My lord,' he said, 'summon your workmen and order them to start digging. Beneath the earth you will find a pool, and that is what keeps your tower from standing.'

The workmen were duly summoned and began to dig. Sure enough, beneath the soil they found a pool which had been making the ground unstable.

Merlin faced the magicians a second time. 'Tell me now, you lying flatterers – what lies beneath the pool?' he demanded. But the magicians remained silent, unable to utter a sound.

'Order the pool to be drained, my lord,' Merlin said to the king. 'At the bottom of it you will discover two hollow stones, and inside each stone you will find a dragon sleeping.'

The king now had great faith in Merlin's words and straight away ordered the pool to be drained. Nothing had ever impressed him as much as this child. All those standing by were equally astonished and sensed that there was something supernatural about the boy.

The labourers began to drain the pool. Before long, two huge stones were revealed and, as the water level dropped, it could be seen that they were, indeed, hollow. When the water had completely drained away, everyone craned forward to see inside the stones. As they watched, two dragons emerged – one white and one red. The dragons approached each other and started to fight. They fought fiercely and bitterly, breathing out such great tongues of flame that Vortigern, looking down, felt he might be standing on the brink of hell itself.

The dragons seemed to be well matched, until suddenly the white one seized the advantage and forced the red one to the edge of the pool. The red dragon, momentarily defeated, became angrier than ever. With its tail lashing furiously it turned on its opponent and attacked with renewed vigour. The white dragon, taken off guard, lost ground and began to retreat. Then it turned and fled, taking refuge once again in the hollow stone.

Vortigern addressed the boy at his side. 'What does this battle of the dragons mean?' he demanded.

Merlin burst into tears as he felt the onset of a prophetic trance. When the trance was fully upon him, he began to speak.

'Alas for the Red Dragon!' he said. 'Its victory will be short-lived, for its end is near. Its caverns will be occupied by the White Dragon, which represents the Saxons, whom you have invited here. The Red Dragon represents the people of Britain who will be overrun by the White One. Terrible devastation will take place: Britain's mountains and valleys will be levelled and her streams will run crimson with blood. Religion will be abolished and the churches ruined. But the oppressed race will be victorious in the end. The Boar of Cornwall will bring relief from the savage invaders, trampling them beneath its feet. The Boar's end will remain a mystery, but the Boar will be loudly applauded by the people of Cornwall and its deeds will provide meat and drink for future story-tellers.'

'London's dignity will be seen at Canterbury and the seventh pastor of York will be visited in Armorica (Brittany). Blood will flow and a terrible famine will afflict mankind. The Red Dragon will grieve for all this, but with a supreme effort it will regain its strength and calamity will fall upon the White One.'

All who heard Merlin's words were astounded by them and looked closely at the king to see if he was angry. But Vortigern was intrigued by the prophecies and allowed the entranced boy to continue.

'Death will snatch away the peoples of every nation,' said Merlin. 'Those who are left will desert their native soil and sow their seeds in foreign lands.'

He then told of the conquest of Ireland and went on to predict many other things, including the arrival of a round halfpenny piece: 'The shape of commerce will be cut in two, and one half will be rounded.' He predicted the sinking of a ship in which the children of a future king (Henry I) would be drowned: 'The lion's cubs will be transformed into fishes of the sea.' He told of future plagues and pestilence: 'The baths at the city of Bath will grow cold and the health-giving waters will breed death. London will mourn the death of twenty thousand...' He spoke of the 'Boar of Commerce' and the 'Ass of Wickedness' and referred, symbolically, to various animals and birds: the eagle (a bird of storm), the raven, owl, fox, wolf, bear and many others. He predicted that unnatural disturbances of nature would occur, evil would stalk the land and men would become salacious and depraved.

'The stars will avert their gaze from these men and alter their accustomed course. The helmet of Mars will attract Venus and cast a shadow, so enraging Mercury that he will overrun his orbit. Orion will bare his sword. The Gemini twins will cease embracing and send Aquarius to the fountains, and the scales of Libra will hang crookedly until Aries props them up with his horns. The tail of Scorpio will shoot lightning and Cancer will do battle with the Sun. Virgo will throw off her maiden modesty and climb on the back of Sagittarius. Finally, with a baleful blast, the winds will do battle together, and the ominous sound they make will echo throughout the heavens.'

When Merlin had made these prophecies, the listeners were more taken aback than ever. They could not pretend to understand all he had said, but they were amazed that one so young should speak in such a manner before the king. Vortigern himself was equally impressed.

'Now I wish to know how my own life will end,' he said. 'What can you tell me of that?'

Merlin replied, 'The fire of vengeance is with Ambrosius and Uther, the sons of Constantine – flee from it if you can. At this very moment they are preparing to leave the coasts of Armorica and sail across the sea. They will make for Britain and subdue the Saxons, whom they detest, but first they intend to shut you up in your tower and burn you alive. Thus the Saxons, whom you summoned to protect you, will ensure your violent end.

'Yet there are two different deaths which threaten you, and I cannot see clearly which of the two you will escape. On one side, the Saxons will ravage your kingdom and attempt to kill you. On the other, Aurelius and Uther, the brothers of Constans, seek revenge upon you for the death of their brother and the betrayal of their father. Find refuge as quickly as you can, for tomorrow they land at Totnes.

'The faces of the Saxons will be bloodied and their leader, Hengist, will be killed. Aurelius Ambrosius will be crowned king. He will bring peace to the people and restore their churches to them, but he himself will be poisoned and his brother, Uther, will succeed him as king. His life too will be cut short by poison, and in this despicable act your own descendants will play a part, after which the Boar of Cornwall will devour them.'

The following morning, as Merlin had predicted, Aurelius Ambrosius and his brother, Uther, put into harbour at Totnes. Vortigern fled to the castle of Ganarew on the River Wye, where he fortified himself against attack.

So how correct was Merlin's prophecy of Vortigern's death? There is little doubt that he was incinerated alive and many believe that the tortuous death took place in his own tower at Dinas Emrys. But did he escape from Ganarew Castle and flee back to his tower? Or was he, in fact, burnt alive by Aurelius Ambrosius in Ganarew Castle? At any event, Vortigern was dead and Aurelius, now the new king, assembled his army and marched northwards in pursuit of Hengist and the Saxons, who had retreated across the Humber.

As he passed through the various regions, Aurelius was saddened to see how desolate they were, but most of all he was grieved to find the churches razed to the ground. 'If I am victorious, I shall restore them,' he vowed.

Hengist, meanwhile, was promising his own men victory in view of their great numbers. He placed his army in a field where he intended to ambush the Britons by attacking them stealthily when they least expected it. But Aurelius, hearing of this plan, marched towards the field more quickly than ever, and once within sight of the enemy, placed his own troops strategically so that they blocked the Saxons' escape in every direction.

At this point Eldol, the Duke of Gloucester, came to the king and told him of Hengist's cowardly attack on the unarmed leaders and nobles during the pretended peace conference with Vortigern.

'Had I not defended myself with a branch, I too would have been a victim at that meeting,' he said. 'As it was, and by the grace of God, I managed to escape with my life. But I would give up the remaining days of that life if I could fight hand to hand with Hengist and have the opportunity to kill him.'

Hengist placed his own troops in position and busied himself among them, giving the men orders and inspiring them to fight and win. When all the companies on both sides were in formation the foremost ranks charged into battle. Blow matched blow and a great deal of blood was shed. Aurelius urged on his Christians, and Hengist encouraged his pagans. Eldol sought the opportunity of a hand-to-hand fight with Hengist, but the Saxon leader, realising he faced defeat from the Britons, withdrew with his men and so the duke failed to achieve his purpose.

Aurelius pursued his enemy, killing or taking into slavery every Saxon man whom he overtook on the way. Hengist formed his troops into ranks again and when Aurelius finally caught up with him and attacked, the battle recommenced violently. The Saxons returned the Britons' attack with great savagery; the ground was wet with blood in every direction, and the screams of the dying on both sides roused the living to further fury.

The Saxons may well have been the victors had not an Armorican cavalry detachment – placed by Aurelius on the flanks to prevent the Saxons escaping – charged into the battle. The Saxons gave ground under this unexpected attack, and were unable to close their ranks successfully again. At this the Britons fought more fiercely than ever, and none more so than Aurelius, their king, who shouted orders and encouragement to his men while dealing out death and injury to the enemy.

Eldol was also fighting brilliantly, but while he dealt fatal blows to all who opposed him, his heart was still set on a personal fight with the Saxon leader. Finally, his chance came. As the companies of troops moved forward, he and Hengist were suddenly brought together in a savage duel.

The two leaders were well matched – and what champions they were! They lunged and thrust at each other mercilessly. Sparks flew from the clashing metal of their swords, as if they created their own thunder and lightning. One moment Eldol appeared to have the advantage, the next moment it seemed to lie with Hengist.

Gorlois, Duke of Cornwall, then moved towards them with his battalion, destroying the enemy ranks as he approached. At the sight of Gorlois, Eldol was inspired with greater confidence and seized hold of Hengist's helmet by the nose-piece. Exerting all his strength, he manged to drag the Saxon leader down, and the fight was over. 'God has granted my prayer!' he shouted joyfully. 'Come men! Down with what remains of these Saxon villains. Victory is in your hands!'

The Britons, meanwhile, redoubled their attack on the Saxons and were victorious. The Saxons took flight and scattered, each man for himself, some fleeing to the cities, some taking refuge in the mountains and forests and others returning to their ships.

Having won his victory, Aurelius ordered that the dead be buried and the wounded be tended. Then he comforted his weary men and told them to rest. Finally, he called his leaders together and asked them to decide what should be done with Hengist.

Eldol's brother, Eldadus the Bishop of Gloucester, spoke loudly and clearly for Hengist's execution.

'Even if everyone present were to vote for this man's freedom, I myself would hack him to pieces,' he declared. 'For didn't Samuel, the prophet, say when he hacked the wicked King Amalek to pieces, "As thy sword has made women childless, so shall I make thy mother childless among women"? I beseech you, do the same to Hengist, for he is another Amalek.'

Therefore Aurelius ordered Hengist to be taken outside the city and executed, and Eldol was allowed to cut off his head personally. Then Aurelius, being a reasonable man, gave instructions for Hengist to be buried and a barrow of earth raised over his body, in keeping with the pagan custom.

Hengist's son, Octa, surrendered to Aurelius at York, with his noblemen. 'My own gods are vanquished and I cannot deny that it is your God who reigns supreme,' he said. Then, handing Aurelius a chain, he continued, 'Accept us and also accept this length of chain. If you cannot grant us mercy, have us bound and punished as you see fit.'

Aurelius was moved by Octa's words and took counsel with his advisors to decide what should be done with the Saxons. The bishop who had pleaded for Hengist's execution now advocated compassion. 'They beg for mercy, so let them have mercy,' said Eldadus, 'Our island of Britain is large enough and in many places uninhabited – let them occupy those spaces and remain our subjects for ever.'

The king agreed to this and took pity on the Saxons, granting them a region on the borders of Scotland and signing a treaty with them. He then set to work rebuilding the metropolitan cathedral at York and gave orders that all the churches devastated by the Saxons should be restored. Once this work was under way he went to London and, calling together all the citizens left alive there, he began the task of rebuilding the city.

From London he ruled his kingdom, renewing laws that had fallen into disuse and restoring the scattered possessions of the dead to their rightful heirs. Next he went to Winchester to restore that town as well, and afterwards – on the advice of Bishop Eldadus – he visited the place that is now called Salisbury.

It was at Salisbury that the barons and earls so treacherously slaughtered by Hengist's Saxons lay buried. As Aurelius looked at the expanse of green turf that was their burial ground, he was moved to tears. However, he quickly told himself that tears were not enough and that he must do something to make the place worthy of remembrance. But what? He thought about this for some time before calling together master carpenters and stonemasons from every region. 'Use your skills to contrive a unique building,' he told them, 'a building that will stand for ever in memory of these distinguished men.'

The craftsmen gave it much thought, but in the end they shook their heads and had to admit themselves defeated. When the Archbishop of the City of the Legions heard about this, he went to King Aurelius with his own suggestion.

'If there is anyone anywhere who is capable of carrying out your plan, it is Vortigern's prophet, Merlin,' he said, 'for there is no one else in your kingdom who has greater skills, either in foreseeing the future or in contriving mechanical devices. Bid Merlin come here and use his talents. Then you shall have a monument that will last!'

Aurelius asked many questions about Merlin, and then sent messengers to various parts of the kingdom to try to find him. He was eventually discovered at one of his favourite haunts: the Galabes Springs at Gwent, in Wales. The messengers explained the king's plan and then led him to Aurelius, who greeted him gladly and ordered him to prophesy the future. 'For I am well disposed to hear some of these marvels,' he said.

Merlin, however, refused to reveal any of them. 'Mysteries of that kind can be told only when there is an urgent need for them,' he said. 'If I were to utter them simply for your entertainment, then the spirit that controls me would forsake me in the hour of need.'

In the same manner he refused all those present who asked him to predict the future. Aurelius accepted this with a good grace and told him of the building he wished to construct.

'If it is your wish to honour the burial-place of these men with a monument that will endure,' said Merlin, 'send for the Dance of the Giants which is on Mount Killare in Ireland. It is a structure of stones which no living man could erect – unless his skill and artistry were quite exceptional. The stones are enormous and there is no one alive who is strong enough to move them. But if they are set up on this site – in a circle, as they are set now in Ireland – then they will stand here for ever.'

At these words Aurelius could not help laughing. 'How is it possible,' he asked, 'that such huge stones can be brought here from a distant country? It is not as if Britain itself is lacking in stones big enough for the job!'

'Do not laugh so lightly, your Majesty,' Merlin replied, 'for I do not speak lightly. In these stones there is a mystery; they are witness to secret rites and bear within them strange healing powers. The giants of old carried them from Africa and set them up in Ireland at a time when they inhabited that land. They did this so that they might prepare baths, at the feet of the stones, for any of their people who fell ill. They would wash the stones with water, the water would pour forth into the baths and those who were sick would be cured. They also mixed the water with a concoction of herbs to heal the wounds of any who were injured. There is not one stone among them that does not have some medicinal property.'

When the Britons heard all this they decided to send for the stones and, if necessary, take arms against the people of Ireland in order to get them. Uther, the king's brother, was chosen to lead the expedition and fifteen thousand men were allocated to him for the task. It was agreed that Merlin should accompany them so that they would have the benefit of his knowledge and advice. The ships were made ready, and with a favourable wind they set sail for Ireland.

At that time, young King Gilloman ruled Ireland. As soon as he heard that the Britons had landed on his shores, he collected a large army together and went to meet them. When he heard the reason for their coming he laughed aloud and turned to those who stood about him.

'I am not surprised that a race of heathens was able to devastate the island of Britain,' he said, 'for the Britons themselves are no more than dull-witted fools. Whoever heard of such folly? Are the stones of Ireland so much better than the stones of Britain that we should be invaded for them? Arm yourselves, men, and defend your country! As long as I live they shall not carry away the smallest fragment of the Giants' Dance.'

Seeing that the Irishmen were only too willing to fight, Uther wasted no time; positioning his own men for the fray, he charged at those who had now declared themselves enemies. The Britons were the better fighters and the battle was brief. Most of the Irish were killed or maimed almost at once and Gilloman was forced to flee for his life.

Triumphantly, Uther and his men marched forward to Mount Killare. When they reached the stone structure known as the Dance of the Giants they gazed at it in wonder and delight, for seldom had they seen anything so impressive. The stones were huge.

As they stood silently staring, Merlin approached them. 'Now,' he said, 'try your utmost to remove these stones. You will soon discover which is the greater advantage – strength or skill.'

At his bidding they set to work in an attempt to dismantle the ring of stones. Some used ropes and cables while others propped scaling ladders against the enormous stones. They worked until they were exhausted but their efforts were futile. They did not succeed in moving the smallest stone so much as a fraction of an inch.

Laughing at their frustration, Merlin began to put together his own mechanical devices. He assembled everything he needed and then, with masterly skill, he brought the great stones down so effortlessly, that the weary men looking on could hardly believe their eyes. Having pulled them down, he ordered the men to carry them to the ships and place them on board. This was eventually achieved and the Britons set sail for home with joyful hearts. Once again they were favoured by a fair wind, and when the ships reached the shores of Britain the stones were unloaded and taken to the burial-site on the plain of Salisbury.

As soon as their arrival was reported to Aurelius, he sent messengers to all the regions of the kingdom, summoning the bishops and abbots to attend the ceremony of re-dedicating the burial-place. They duly arrived on the appointed day, whereupon Aurelius set the crown upon his head and celebrated the Whitsuntide festival in royal fashion, announcing that the next three days would be a holiday so that the festivities could continue. During this time he gave land to those who had no holdings of their own, as a reward for the work they had done in his service.

When he had bestowed these honours and dealt with various other matters, Aurelius ordered Merlin to set up around the burial-place the Giants' Dance, which he had brought from Ireland. Merlin obeyed, placing the stones in a circle on the perimeter of the burial-ground so that they were arranged in exactly the way that they had been on Mount Killare. Everyone present could see that Merlin's artistry easily outmatched any brute strength.

Meanwhile, Vortigern's son, Pascentius, was in Germany, rallying every knight in that kingdom to take up arms against Aurelius Ambrosius to avenge his father. He promised the German soldiers huge sums of money if they would help him to conquer Britain, and the young men were quite willing to be bribed. Pascentius fitted out a large fleet and sailed to the northern parts of Britain, where he and his 'bought' army proceeded to lay waste to the land. When reports of this reached Aurelius he assembled his own army and marched to challenge the invaders. They accepted the challenge readily and battle commenced, but once again the Britons proved themselves to be the superior fighters, and the Germans were forced to take flight.

Pascentius, having been compelled to run away, did not dare return to Germany. Instead, he set sail for Ireland, to be warmly greeted by King Gilloman, who was still smarting from his defeat by Uther and the loss of the Giants' Dance. The two men signed a treaty of alliance, fitted out their ships and set sail for Britain, where they landed and made for the city of St David's, in Wales.

As soon as this was known, Uther assembled an army and marched into Wales to do battle with them on behalf of his brother, Aurelius, who lay sick in Winchester. Pascentius, Gilloman and the Saxons who had joined them were delighted when they heard this, for with Aurelius ill they felt they could more easily conquer his kingdom.

While they were discussing the situation, a Saxon called Eopa came to Pascentius and asked what reward he would give to the man who killed Aurelius for him.

'If only I could find a man who would resolve to do that,' said Pascentius, 'I would give him a thousand pounds in silver and a life-time's loyalty and affection. And should I be fortunate enough to gain the crown of Britain, I would make him a general in my army. This much I swear on oath.'

'I have learned to speak the British tongue,' said Eopa, 'and I know the habits of the people well. Furthermore, I have some knowledge of medicine. If you will swear to fulfil your promise, I will assume the guise of a Christian and a Briton and gain access to the king by pretending to be a leech (doctor). Then I shall pretend to give Aurelius some medicine and mix a potion that will kill him. So that I may gain an audience with him more readily, I will disguise myself as a devout monk.'

Pascentius very willingly made an agreement with the man, confirming on oath to give him everything that he had promised. So Eopa shaved off his beard, had his head tonsured and donned the habit of a monk. Then, laden with pots of medicines and drugs to give credibility to his disguise, he set off for Winchester and, on arriving in the town, immediately offered his services to the king's household. No one could have been more welcome than a doctor at that time. He was taken to the king straight away, whereupon he promised to restore Aurelius to health if he would only swallow the medicines mixed for him.

Eopa was ordered to mix a potion immediately, and this he did – offering it to the king, who drained it in one gulp. When Aurelius had swallowed the fatal mixture, Eopa told him to cover himself up warmly and go to sleep; the treacherous Saxon knew that this would make the poison work more effectively. The king, unsuspecting, did as his false medic advised and went to sleep, thinking to speed his recovery. But the poison soon ran through his veins, bringing death to Aurelius as he slept. Eopa, meanwhile, slipped quietly from the court and made sure he was never seen in the vicinity again.

While this drama was being enacted at Winchester, something even more dramatic was occurring in the heavens. A star of spectacular size and brilliance appeared, from which shone a single beam of light. At the end of this beam was a ball of fire that spread out in the shape of a dragon. From the dragon's mouth issued two further rays of light: one seeming to spread itself beyond the regions of Gaul (France) and the other turning towards the Irish Sea and splitting into seven smaller rays.

All who saw this star were filled with wonder and fear. Uther, the king's brother, who we left marching into Wales with his army, saw the star and halted his men – as terrified by the sight as everyone else. He summoned various wizards to tell him what the star portended, and among them he called Merlin who had accompanied the army to offer his advice. 'Tell me,' said Uther, when the magician stood before him, 'what does the appearance of this star signify?'

Merlin burst into tears, as he usually did when visited by his entrancing spirit. Then he drew a long breath. 'O, irreparable loss!' he cried. 'The people of Britain are orphaned! Our renowned king, Aurelius Ambrosius, is dead – and by his death we shall all die if God does not help us. Therefore hasten, most noble Duke Uther, hasten forward and do not hesitate to do battle with your enemies. Victory will be yours and you will be king of all Britain. The star shines for you, personally, and the fiery dragon under the star is your own sign. Moreover, the ray of light that stretches forward to the regions of Gaul signifies that a son shall be born to you. He will be a ruler of unsurpassed greatness whose power will extend over all the regions that lie beneath the ray. The other ray of light signifies a daughter whose sons and grandsons will succeed, one after the other, to the throne of Britain.'

Uther was not convinced that Merlin's prophecies were true, but nevertheless he continued to advance towards the enemy, for his army was now no more than half a day's march from St David's City. His approach was reported to Gilloman, Pascentius and the Saxons who were with them and immediately they marched out to meet him, ready to do battle.

The opposing forces met at such close quarters that hand-to-hand combat took place and, inevitably, soldiers were slaughtered on either side. The battle raged until the daylight was almost gone, by which time the Britons were proving stronger. Finally, with the slaying of Gilloman and Pascentius, Uther was victorious. The barbarians turned and fled from the Christians, who gave chase, killing many of the Saxons as they ran for the safety of their ships.

Uther thanked God for his victory and then hurried towards Winchester. On the way he was greeted with the sorry news of the king's death. The messengers who brought the news told him that Aurelius was to be buried by the bishops in the place he had chosen – the burial-ground within the stone ring of the Giants' Dance. When they heard of the king's death, all the bishops, abbots and clergy of the diocese of Winchester assembled in the town and honoured him with a funeral that befitted a great monarch. Then they took his body to the plain of Salisbury and, with much pomp, laid him to rest in the cemetery he had prepared for the Christian noblemen and in which he had ordained he should be buried himself.

After the funeral of his brother, Uther took the crown into his own safe-keeping and called together all the clergy and people of his kingdom. They agreed unanimously that he should be their ruler and, accordingly, he was officially crowned King of Britain. Remembering Merlin's explanation of the extraordinary star, Uther ordered two dragons to be made in gold, exactly like the one he had seen in the beam of light from the star.

The dragons were fashioned with remarkable craftsmanship exactly as Uther desired. When they were complete he presented one as a gift to the cathedral church of Winchester, and the other he kept to carry with him into battle. From that time forward he was known as Uther Pendragon (pendragon meaning 'a dragon's head'), a title accorded to him because of Merlin's prophecy that he would become king by means of the dragon. Merlin's other prophecy – that a ruler of unsurpassed greatness would be born to Uther – referred, of course, to the coming of King Arthur.

Arthur

From Sir Thomas Malory's *Morte D'Arthur*, Book I
'The Book of Merlin and of Uther Pendragon and his Son Arthur'
and Book II 'The Book of Balin le Savage'.

**KING ARTHUR'S BIRTH
AND ADOPTION**

THE SWORD IN THE STONE

THE LADY OF THE LAKE

THE TRAGEDY OF BALIN AND BALAN

SIR ECTOR: Now I understand that you must be
king of this land.
ARTHUR: Wherefore I? And for what cause?
SIR ECTOR: Sir, there should never no man have
drawn out this sword, but he that shall be
rightwise king of this land.

THE BOOK OF MERLIN, III

The Coming of Arthur

 hen Uther Pendragon ruled as king, he and the Cornish Duke of Tintagel were frequently at war. Eventually, Uther decided that the hostilities must cease, and he summoned the duke and his wife to his own castle.

His hospitality had the desired effect, and the two great men were reconciled at last. There was, however, an unexpected complication. Igraine, the duke's wife, was a very beautiful woman. As soon as Uther set eyes on her he desired her passionately. He made this known to the lady, but she – being a good and loyal wife – refused his advances and informed her husband. 'It seems the only reason we were sent for was so that I should be dishonoured,' she told him. 'And if you will take my advice, husband, we shall leave here immediately and ride through the night to our own castle.'

The duke agreed and they left quickly, without informing the king or any of his servants of their departure. When Uther discovered that they had gone he was furious and summoned his privy council to inform them of the duke's discourtesy. The councillors advised him to send a royal summons to the duke, demanding that he and his wife return at once.

'If he will not come at your command,' said the chief councillor, 'then you have no option but to declare war on him.'

Messengers were dispatched to Cornwall with the royal command and Uther waited anxiously for the duke's reply. When it came, it was brief: neither he nor his wife would come to the king. This further incensed Uther, who sent his messengers back, instructing the duke to furnish himself with men and stores, for within forty days Uther, the king, would fetch him out of the strongest castle he possessed.

On receiving this warning the duke fortified his two strongest castles, those of Tintagel and Terrabil. He put Igraine, for safety, into Tintagel Castle, which he considered to be impregnable, and then positioned himself in the castle of Terrabil, which had many escape routes should he need them.

Uther arrived with a huge army and laid siege to Castle Terrabil, setting up his camp there. Immediately the two sides went to war and a great many men were killed. But in the midst of the battle, Uther fell sick and was unable to continue fighting. A noble knight called Sir Ulfius came speedily to the king's side and asked what ailed him.

'I am sick from anger,' Uther replied, 'yet that is not the main reason for my malady.'

'Then what, sire?' asked the knight.

'I am sick,' gasped the king, 'for the love of Igraine. Her beauty haunts me day and night and I am a broken man.'

'Then, my lord,' said Ulfius, 'I shall seek out Merlin, for he will surely find a remedy to ease your heart.'

Ulfius departed immediately to look for the magician, and while he was searching for him he chanced upon a beggar attired in dirty rags. 'Who is it you seek?' asked the beggar.

Ulfius made to pass him contemptuously. 'I have little reason to tell you!' he replied.

'I know it is Merlin whom you seek,' said the beggar. 'Therefore look no further, for I am Merlin. And if King Uther will reward me by granting what I ask of him – which, in truth, will be more to his benefit and honour than to mine – I shall grant his dearest wish.' Ulfius halted, impressed by the man's speech. 'Ride on,' said Merlin, 'and I will follow close behind.'

So Ulfius, cheered by these words, rode to the king and told him that he had found Merlin.

'Where is he?' asked Uther.

'He will be here shortly, sir,' Ulfius replied, and even as he spoke, he realised that Merlin stood at the entrance to the king's pavilion and that he was no longer wearing the tattered clothes of a beggar. Uther greeted the magician warmly.

'Your Majesty,' said Merlin, 'I know your heart's desire, and if you give me your royal oath that you will grant my request, then I promise that you shall have your wish.'

The king gave his oath at once. 'Sir,' said Merlin, 'this is my request: you shall father a child by Igraine and, when it is born, you will hand it over to me to rear and nourish in the manner I choose, for this will be to your honour and to the child's advantage in every way.'

'I will do exactly as you ask,' the king promised.

'Then make yourself ready,' said Merlin, 'for tonight you shall sleep with Igraine in the castle of Tintagel.'

The king's heart leapt with joy, yet he found Merlin's words difficult to believe. 'But how?' he asked.

'You shall enter the castle in the likeness of Igraine's husband, the Duke of Tintagel', Merlin told him. 'Ulfius shall look like Sir Brastias, who is a knight of the duke's, and I shall take on the aspect of Sir Jordains, who is another of the duke's knights.' Then he warned the king to be cautious. 'Speak as little as possible and do not ask many questions of Igraine, nor of her men. Say you are indisposed and do not rise from your bed until I come for you in the morning.'

Everything was done as Merlin had said, for by his extraordinary powers the change was accomplished. But the Duke of Tintagel saw the king ride away from his siege camp at Terrabil, so he left the castle in order to mount an attack on the king's men while their leader was absent. In the affray that followed the duke was mortally wounded and died before Uther even reached the castle of Tintagel. The king, having the appearance of the duke, gained access to the castle and to his beloved Igraine and lay with her some three hours after her husband's death.

The following morning, Merlin – still in the likeness of the duke's knight, Sir Jordains – came to Uther and told him to prepare to leave immediately. So Uther kissed Igraine and departed.

Later in the day, messengers arrived at Tintagel with news of the duke's death. They were able to tell his wife the exact hour of his death. Realising that this was the time at which the man she had thought to be her husband had been making love to her, Igraine marvelled at the night's events and was more than a little perplexed. However, being a wise lady, as well as a good and loyal wife, she mourned her lord discreetly and said nothing.

Merlin's magic wore off quickly and Uther resumed his own appearance. Then his barons came to him and pleaded that he should now be reconciled with the lady Igraine. The king was only too willing to be reconciled with the woman he loved, so he allowed the noble Sir Ulfius to arrange a meeting between them. Ulfius negotiated tactfully on Uther's behalf and, eventually, the meeting took place.

'Now we should look further ahead,' Ulfius told the knights and noblemen. 'Our king is a strong and vigorous knight and he is still wifeless. Lady Igraine is very beautiful and we would all be delighted if he were to make her his queen.' Then he added, with a twinkle, 'I think it may not displease the king to do so, either!'

The idea met with everyone's approval and it was put to the king who agreed very willingly. Igraine assented graciously and the marriage was arranged quickly but with much celebration. After he had made Igraine his queen, King Uther requested that her young daughters should also be married: Margawse to King Lot of Orkney and Elaine to King Nentres of Garlot. The youngest daughter, Morgan le Fay, was put to school in a nunnery, where she learnt so well that she became a great scholar of necromancy.

As Merlin had foreseen, Igraine had conceived a child when Uther lay with her in the likeness of her husband. Now, as the time for her child's birth approached, Uther spoke to Igraine about it for the first time. 'Tell me,' he said, 'for as your husband it is my right to know – who is the father of the child you are carrying?' Igraine hesitated, embarrassed. 'Come, Igraine,' said the king. 'Don't be distressed, just tell me the truth. I swear by my faith I shall love you the more for it.'

'Then, sir,' she replied, 'I shall tell you the truth. The very night my lord the duke was killed – almost at the hour of his death, in fact – a man who appeared to be my husband came into the castle at Tintagel, and with him came two knights who looked exactly like the duke's own men, Brastias and Jordains. I received him as I should receive my husband and that night, as I shall answer to God, the child was conceived.'

'I know you are telling the truth,' said Uther and he took the queen tenderly in his arms. 'It was I who came to you that night in the likeness of your husband. You have nothing to fear, for I am the father of your child.' Then he told her how Merlin had devised the plan and made it possible, and the queen was delighted to learn that Uther was the father.

Soon after this, Merlin himself came to the king. 'Sir,' he said, 'it is now time to arrange for the fostering of your child.'

'Whatever you say, I shall abide by it,' Uther replied.

'Well,' said Merlin, 'I know a lord who is a faithful and honourable knight and I propose to place the child in his care. His name is Sir Ector and he has land in both England and Wales. Send for him and ask him to give his own child to another woman to foster so that his wife can undertake the nourishing of yours. When your child is born, give it to me, unchristened, at the postern gate of your castle.'

Uther agreed and Sir Ector was summoned. He vowed to care for the child just as the king desired, and Uther granted him many rewards. When the child – a boy – was born, his mother wrapped him in rich cloth of gold and the king summoned two knights and two ladies to take him to the postern gate of the castle. 'Deliver him into the care of the man whom you will find waiting there,' he commanded.

And so the baby was handed to Merlin who took him to the good Sir Ector, where a holy man was called to christen him and to name him Arthur. It was not unusual in those days for the children of noblemen to be reared by foster-parents, and so Sir Ector's wife gladly took the baby to her own breast and suckled him.

Within two years of his son's adoption, King Uther fell sick, and while he was ill his enemies advanced and attacked his men, killing a great number of them. Merlin came to the king and remonstrated with him.

'Sir,' he said, 'you cannot afford to lie here out of sight. You must be seen on the battlefield, even if you have to be taken there in a horse-litter. You will never get the better of your enemies while you are invisible, but if you are seen on the field, then you shall have the victory.'

The king did as Merlin advised. He was carried towards his enemies in a horse-litter at the head of his army. When they reached St Albans they were met by a mighty force from the north and battle commenced. Two knights were particularly outstanding in their deeds of bravery that day – Sir Ulfius and the Duke of Tintagel's former knight, Sir Brastias.

King Uther's men overcame the army from the north, killing many of the warriors and putting the rest to flight. The king was then taken to London where he celebrated his victory with great joy, but afterwards his sickness became worse and he lay speechless for three days and three nights. His noblemen were deeply concerned and asked Merlin what could be done for him.

'There is no further remedy,' said Merlin sadly. 'God must now have His will. But come before your king tomorrow morning and I promise that he shall speak to you.'

On the following morning all the barons assembled before the king, and Merlin addressed Uther. 'Sir,' he said, 'shall your son Arthur be king after you, and hold those privileges that accompany the crown of England?'

King Uther turned to the magician, and although he was now very weak indeed, he spoke so that all those present could hear him. 'I give my son God's blessing and my own,' he said. 'I bid him pray for my soul, and claim the crown that is rightfully his.' With those words, King Uther Pendragon of England drew his final breath. He was buried with such ceremony as befitted an illustrious king, and Queen Igraine and all his barons mourned him with great sorrow.

For many years after Uther's death, the kingdom was without a monarch and in great jeopardy, for every lord with sufficient men at his command armed himself for battle, and many of those lords fully expected to be made king of England. Merlin went to the Archbishop of Canterbury and advised him to summon all lords of the realm and gentlemen of arms to London. He told him to insist that they either come before Christmas or be excommunicated. 'For wasn't our Lord born on that night?' said Merlin. 'And won't he in his mercy, as he is king of all mankind, show by some miracle who should now be king of England?'

The archbishop could not deny that this might be so, and he took Merlin's advice and sent for all the lords and gentlemen of arms, instructing them to arrive in London by Christmas Eve. They came obediently, doubtless hoping that any miracle would show to their advantage, and many of them confessed their sins in order to purify themselves and make their prayers more acceptable to God. They all assembled in the great church of St Paul's, to pray together before the dawn of Christmas Day.

When morning prayers and the first mass were finished, it seemed as if a miracle had indeed occurred, for an enormous square stone had appeared in the churchyard. From an anvil set in the centre of this stone there stood a fine sword, on the hilt of which, in letters of gold, were the words: 'Whoso pulleth out the sword of this stone and anvil, is righteous king born of all England.'

The people who saw this marvelled at it and went to tell the archbishop. 'I command you to keep within the church and to pray,' he told them sternly. 'And no man shall touch the sword until all the masses have been said.'

When the masses were completed, all the lords went to look at the stone and the sword and read the inscription that was on the hilt of the sword. Some of them attempted to remove the stone from the anvil to prove that they were born to be king but, pull and wrench as they might, not one of them was successful.

'The man who shall remove the sword is not yet among us,' said the archbishop. 'But never doubt that God will make him known to us, and it is my counsel that we appoint ten knights of good repute and give the sword into their keeping.'

This was done, and it was announced that every man who felt himself worthy of winning the sword could attempt to do so. The barons were instructed to arrange jousts and tournaments to take place on New Year's Day, and every knight who took part in the jousts or tourneys would be allowed to compete for the sword. The archbishop felt this to be a good thing as it meant that the knights and commoners would be together in one place, and he trusted God to make it clear to them who should win the sword and be their rightful king.

On New Year's Day, when the church service was over, the barons rode on to the field, some to joust by tilting with lances at a single opponent and some to tourney, which was to ride to combat in the tournaments with other knights. It happened that Sir Ector – who owned estates in the vicinity of London – rode to the jousts with his son, Sir Kay, and young Arthur, his adopted son. Sir Kay was particularly anxious to acquit himself well at the jousts, as he had only very recently been made a knight. It was therefore with great consternation that he discovered he had failed to bring his sword with him! Remembering that he had left it at his father's lodging, he begged young Arthur to fetch it for him.

'I'll go at once!' said Arthur willingly, and rode as fast as he could to the lodging. But when he reached the house he found it was locked and no amount of hammering on the door brought a response, for everyone had gone to watch the jousting. Arthur was dismayed at the thought of returning to Sir Kay without his sword – and then he had an idea. 'I'll ride to the churchyard,' he said to himself, 'and get for Kay that sword that is sticking up out of the stone. For I swear that my brother shall not be without a sword on this day of all days!'

So Arthur rode to the churchyard, where he dismounted and tied his horse to a stile. A tent had been erected for the stone and sword, but there was no one there as all the knights were at the jousting. Arthur approached the stone, took hold of the sword by its handle and with one swift movement pulled it from the anvil.

He remounted his horse, rode with all speed to Sir Kay and handed him the sword. As soon as Kay set eyes on it he knew it was the one from the stone, and so he rode with it to his father. 'Look, sir!' he cried, 'I have here the sword of the stone – therefore I must be the king of England!'

When Sir Ector saw the sword he told Kay and Arthur to ride with him back to the churchyard. Then all three went into the church and Sir Ector made his son swear upon a holy book how he came by the sword. Kay blushed, humiliated, but answered at once. 'From my brother, Arthur, sir, for he brought it to me.'

Sir Ector turned to young Arthur. 'How did you come into possession of this sword?' he demanded.

'I will tell you, sir,' said Arthur, beginning to wonder if he had done something wrong. 'When I went home to get my brother's sword there was no one in the house and the door was locked.

I thought Kay could not possibly go swordless for the jousting, so I came here quickly and pulled this one from the stone.'

'Did you find any knights here with the sword?' asked Sir Ector.

'No, sir.'

'Then,' said Sir Ector in amazement, 'I have to believe that you are king of this land.'

'Why me?' cried Arthur, even more amazed. 'For what reason?'

'God has decreed it so,' replied Sir Ector. 'For no man can draw this sword from the stone unless he is the rightful king of England. Now, let me see if you can put the sword back where it was and pull it out again.'

'It is not difficult,' said Arthur, and he replaced the sword in the anvil. Sir Ector attempted to pull it out but was unable to do so.

'Now you try,' Sir Ector said to Kay. The young knight stepped forward and pulled at the sword with all his strength but, like his father, he was unable to move it.

'Now you shall attempt it,' Sir Ector said to Arthur.

'Most willingly!' the boy replied, and he pulled the sword out with ease. Sir Ector and Sir Kay immediately fell to their knees before him. 'Oh, my own dear father and brother!' cried Arthur, distressed. 'Why do you kneel to me?'

'No, no, my lord, Arthur, it is not so,' said Sir Ector. 'I was never your father, nor of your blood, but I see now that you are of even higher blood than I thought.' And then he told Arthur how, as a baby, Arthur had been entrusted to his wife's care, after being delivered to him by Merlin.

Arthur was dismayed to learn that Sir Ector was not his father, for he loved him dearly. Sir Ector, too, was deeply moved. 'Will you be my good and gracious lord when you are king?' he asked solemnly.

'How could I not be?' cried Arthur. 'I am more beholden to you than to any other man in the world, and to my good lady and mother your wife, who has kept me and fostered me as one of her own all these years. Should it ever be God's will that I am king as you say, then I shall give you anything you ask for. I shall not fail you. God forbid that I should fail you!'

'Sir, I shall ask only one thing of you,' said Sir Ector, 'and it is this – that you make my son, your foster brother Sir Kay, seneschal (steward) of all your lands.'

'That shall be done,' Arthur promised, 'and more, for by my faith, I swear that no man but Kay shall hold that office for as long as we both live.' They then went to the archbishop, and Sir Ector told him how Arthur had achieved the sword and in what circumstances.

On the twelfth day after Christmas all the barons came to the churchyard and a great many attempted to pull the sword from the stone but none was successful. Arthur was commanded to withdraw the sword again, and when he did so a number of the lords became very angry, complaining that it was most unfair to all of them if their realms were to be governed by a mere chit of a boy who was not even of royal blood!

There was so much quarrelling among the barons that they eventually decided to postpone any further attempts to remove the sword until Candlemass (February 2), when they would all meet again in the churchyard. Meanwhile, the ten knights of good repute were instructed to watch over the sword by night and day. They did so in good faith, ensuring that five of them were always on duty in the pavilion that had been set up over the stone.

At Candlemass the barons assembled again, and many other great lords also came to the churchyard determined to try their skill at winning the sword. But none of them succeeded except Arthur, who did at Candlemass what he had done at Christmas, and pulled the sword from the stone with ease. Again the barons were incensed and decided to postpone the proceedings until the high feast of Easter.

Needless to say, when they all reassembled in the churchyard at Easter exactly the same thing happened: no one but young Arthur could lift the sword from the stone. And still some of them were indignant and refused to accept this evidence. So they postponed the decision once more until the feast of Pentecost.

At this point Merlin, fearing for Arthur's safety, spoke to the Archbishop of Canterbury and asked him to assign those noble knights who had been most trusted by King Uther Pendragon to Arthur for his protection. Thus, many of King Uther's best-loved knights came to be in Arthur's presence at all times; they included Sir Ulfius and Sir Brastias, a knight called Sir Boudwine, and – at Arthur's request – his own foster-brother, Sir Kay.

When the feast of Pentecost arrived, all manner of men assembled in the churchyard to attempt the feat that could make them king. But again, it was only Arthur who succeeded, pulling the sword from the stone within sight of all the lords and commoners. And it was the commoners who now called out in his favour. 'We will have Arthur for our king! We shall not delay any longer! It is God's will that he shall be our king!' they cried, and then they all knelt down and begged Arthur's mercy because they had denied him for so long. He forgave them graciously and, taking the sword between his two hands, he offered it up to the altar where the archbishop was standing.

So young Arthur became king of all England and promised at his coronation to be true to his people and to stand for justice as long as he lived. He summoned the barons who had refused to accept his sovereignty and charged them to serve him as they should. Then, with firm resolve, he prepared to take the weight of a whole kingdom upon his youthful shoulders.

The Knight of the Two Swords

 ing Arthur kept his promise to Sir Ector and made his foster-brother, Sir Kay, seneschal of all England. Then he made Sir Ulfius his chamberlain and Sir Brastias warden of the north, for it was from the north that he was most threatened by his enemies.

It was inevitable that such a youthful ruler should make mistakes, and Arthur's first misunderstanding arose very soon after his coronation. He had gone to Wales and arranged a great feast for Pentecost to be held in the city of Caerleon, in Gwent. He was pleasantly surprised because so many kings and noblemen attended his feast: King Lot of Orkney came with five hundred knights, King Urience of Gore with four hundred, King Nentres of Garlot with seven hundred, and the young King of Scotland brought with him six hundred knights.

King Arthur welcomed the visitors joyfully and, thinking they had come to show their love and respect, he sent valuable gifts to all the kings and their knights. The kings, however, were insulted to be offered gifts by 'a beardless boy who was born of low blood' and sent word back to say they would not accept them and had come only to give Arthur the gift of a sharp sword between the neck and shoulders.

When this message was delivered to Arthur, he took the advice of his barons and fortified himself in a strong tower with five hundred good men of arms. The visiting kings then laid siege to the tower but Arthur – being well supplied with provisions – was able to withstand the siege. Within fifteen days Merlin came to the city of Caerleon and the besieging kings asked him for what reason 'that beardless boy, Arthur' was made king.

'I shall tell you the reason,' Merlin replied, 'it is because he is King Uther Pendragon's son.'

'Then he is a bastard!' they cried.

'Not so,' said Merlin, 'for he was conceived immediately after the death of Igraine's husband, the Duke of Tintagel, and thirteen days later King Uther Pendragon married Igraine. Therefore I can prove that he is no bastard, and however much you try to deny it, he shall be the King of England and overcome all his enemies. He shall rule Wales, Ireland, Scotland and many other realms as well.'

Some of the kings marvelled at Merlin's words and were convinced that he spoke the truth, others – King Lot among them – laughed at him and called him a witch. But Merlin advised Arthur to face these enemies, assuring him that he would overcome them, and when some of the enemy knights came over to King Arthur's side, it greatly encouraged him.

Merlin's prophecy proved true, and from then on he counselled young King Arthur through many of his battles. Yet he did not always advise him to fight; there were times when he thought the exuberant young king too eager to kill and cautioned him to be more merciful. 'Have you not done enough?' Merlin demanded on one occasion. 'Of sixty thousand soldiers you have left alive barely fifteen thousand! It is time to call a halt.'

Some years later one of Arthur's mistakes had tragic and far-reaching consequences, and it was a mistake born of ignorance. He had ridden into the city of Caerleon and there he was visited by Margawse – King Lot's wife – who came to him with her four sons, among whom was Gawain – later to become one of

King Arthur's most outstanding knights. Margawse presented herself as a messenger, but in reality she had been sent by her husband to spy on King Arthur's court and she came splendidly attired. She was, in any case, a very beautiful lady. King Arthur was overwhelmed by desire and made love to her, having no idea that she was his half-sister and that their union was an act of incest.

Margawse remained with King Arthur for one month and then departed. When she had left he had a most disturbing dream. He dreamt that large numbers of griffins and serpents invaded his kingdom, burning and slaughtering everyone in the land. He fought them and they wounded him dreadfully but, in the end, he overcame them and killed them all. When the king awoke he felt depressed and filled with a strange foreboding. In order to dispel this mood, he arranged with his knights to go hunting.

His quarry was a large hart that he saw in the forest and which he pursued so hard and so long that his horse fell dead beneath him. His yeoman brought him another horse and the hart was ambushed and slain. But still Arthur felt the strange mood upon him and he sat down beside a fountain, deep in thought.

As he sat there alone, he heard a sound like the baying of thirty hounds and saw coming towards him the strangest beast he had ever seen in his life. It went to the fountain to drink and Arthur realised that the noise came from its belly – yet while the beast was drinking its belly was silent. When it had drunk enough it left the fountain and the terrible noise filled the air once more. This was the extraordinary Questing Beast. It was followed by a king called Pellinore, who swore to Arthur that he would achieve his quest and slay the beast, or die himself in the attempt. King Pellinore followed the beast for the rest of his days but he never did catch it!

After the beast and King Pellinore had departed, Arthur continued to sit by the fountain and there Merlin came to him

Merlin spellbound by his lover Vivien (Nimue in Malory) from *The Idylls of the King* (Eleanor Fortescue Brickdale) *opposite*

and told him that God was displeased with him because he had slept with his own sister. 'And by her you shall have a child who will destroy you and all the knights of your kingdom!' said the magician.

Arthur refused to believe this until Queen Igraine – who was his mother and also the mother of Margawse – was brought before him and told him the truth about his parentage. Arthur knew he was not Sir Ector's son, but now for the first time he met his mother and learnt that King Uther Pendragon was his father. He forgave Igraine for not coming forward sooner, and mother and son embraced each other fondly. Then King Arthur held a feast of celebration that lasted for eight days.

Shortly afterwards, Arthur found himself in hand-to-hand combat with a knight of unusual skill. The knight struck at Arthur's sword with such force that he shattered it, and would probably have treated Arthur's head in the same way had Merlin not intervened. The magician put the knight into a deep sleep and rescued Arthur, who was bleeding dreadfully.

When King Arthur's wounds were healed, he lamented the fact that he no longer had a sword. 'No matter,' said Merlin. 'Nearby is a sword that shall be yours.'

He took the king to a wide lake where, far out in the water, a raised arm clothed in white samite (silk interwoven with gold) held aloft a sword of remarkable craftsmanship. 'There!' said Merlin. 'That is the sword of which I spoke.'

At that moment, a lady appeared at the point where the lake flowed into a channel. 'What damsel is that?' asked the king.

'That is the Lady of the Lake,' Merlin replied, 'and if you ask her graciously, she will give you the sword.'

Guinevere and her ladies in waiting from *The Idylls of the King* (Eleanor Fortescue Brickdale) *opposite*

They approached the Lady of the Lake, Arthur greeted her with great courtesy and then asked her to whom the sword belonged. 'I wish it were mine,' he said, 'for I have no sword.'

'It is mine, sir,' said the damsel, 'and if you will give me a gift when I ask for it, you shall have the sword.'

'By my faith,' cried King Arthur, 'I will give you any gift that you desire!'

'You will see a barge among the rushes,' said the maiden. 'Row yourself out to the sword and take it, with the scabbard. I shall ask for my gift when the time is right.'

So King Arthur and Merlin rowed out to the sword and the king took it, with its scabbard – whereupon the arm and hand disappeared beneath the water.

'Which do you like better, the sword or the scabbard?' Merlin asked.

'Why, the sword of course!' Arthur replied, surprised that he should be asked such a question, for the sword was magnificent.

'Then you are unwise,' said Merlin, 'for the scabbard is worth ten of the sword. While you have the scabbard on you, you shall lose no blood, however badly you are wounded. Keep it with you always.'

King Arthur and Merlin rode into Caerleon. The king was greeted by his knights who, hearing of his many adventures and brave deeds, were very happy to have such a leader. But the king could not feel happy, for May Day was now some weeks past and Merlin had told him that the child who was destined to destroy him would be born on that day.

King Arthur resolved to take action. He sent for all the children who had been born to lords and ladies on May Day and instructed their parents, on pain of death, to hand them to his messengers. They were put into a ship and cast out to sea;

among them was Mordred whom Arthur had fathered and who was the son of King Lot's wife, Margawse.

It happened that the ship foundered and was wrecked on some rocks below a castle. Most of the babies perished, but Mordred was washed up on to the shore alive, where he was found by a good man who took him into his care and reared him. Many noblemen were angry and distressed at the loss of their children, but a number of them blamed Merlin more than Arthur and so – out of fear or loyalty – they held their peace.

Meanwhile Rience, a king of North Wales, had raised a large army to march against King Arthur. He had already encroached upon the king's land and was slaughtering his people. King Arthur called for all lords, knights and gentlemen of arms to gather in the castle Camelot, where he would convene a general council and hold jousts.

The noblemen came as instructed and suitable accommodation was found for them all. Then a lady arrived with a message for the king. As she removed her fur mantle, everyone could see that she wore a splendid sword, the weight of which threatened almost to topple her.

'Lady,' said the king in surprise, 'for what reason do you wear that mighty sword? It hardly becomes you!'

'I will tell you the reason,' the lady replied. 'This sword causes me great sorrow and discomfort, but I shall only be rid of it if a good knight can draw it from the scabbard. He must be honourable in character and action, without wickedness, treachery or deceit; only such a knight may draw the sword from its sheath. I have been to King Rience, for I was told I should find virtuous knights there, but he and all his knights have tried to draw the sword and none has succeeded.'

'Why, this is amazing!' said King Arthur. 'And if it is so, then I will try to draw out the sword myself. I do not presume to think I am the best knight, but I will try as an example to my barons so that they may attempt it after me.'

King Arthur took hold of the sword and pulled at it eagerly, but it would not come out. 'Sir,' said the lady, 'you do not need to pull half so hard, for whoever removes the sword shall do so with little effort.'

'You speak wisely,' said the king. 'And now let me see each of my knights attempt it.'

The king's knights then tried to draw the sword, each in turn, but none could succeed. The lady was deeply distressed and loudly bemoaned the fact that no one could help her. 'Alas!' she cried, 'I was sure that in this court at Camelot I would find the best knights, without stain or dishonour.'

'By my faith, here are knights as good as any in the world!' King Arthur replied with spirit. 'But none has had the good fortune to help you, and for that I am truly sorry.'

However, there was a poor knight from Northumberland with King Arthur at that time; his name was Balin le Savage, and he had been a prisoner for more than six months after slaying a knight who was cousin to the king. Because they knew him to be a good man and were convinced of his innocence, some of the barons had managed to have him released. Now, silent and unobserved, he had come into the court to watch the knights' attempts to remove the sword. His heart beat fast, for he longed to try for the sword as the other knights did, but being poor and so meanly arrayed he did not step forward. In his heart, however, he felt as confident of success as any man there, and as the lady took her leave of King Arthur and his knights, Balin could contain himself no longer. He called out to her, 'Lady! I pray you, allow me to attempt to take the sword! I may be poorly clothed, but in my heart I know I am as capable of success as any other knight present.'

The lady turned to look at Balin and saw in his eyes that he spoke the truth, yet he was so shabbily dressed that she could not believe he was pure enough. 'Sir,' she replied, 'I do not need to suffer further pain and I cannot think that you could succeed where others have failed.'

'Ah, fair damsel,' said Balin, 'honour and fine qualities are not always reflected in a man's clothes. A knight's good character and worthiness are worn within himself, and may never be recognised at all if he is always to be judged by his apparel.'

'By God, you speak the truth!' said the lady, abashed. 'Therefore you may attempt to draw the sword.'

So Balin took hold of the sword and withdrew it easily. King Arthur and his lords marvelled at his triumph, although many of the knights present were angry to think that a poor man had succeeded where they had failed – some even suggested that he had not achieved the sword by his own prowess, but by witchcraft.

The lady, however, was delighted. 'Truly,' she said, 'here is an excellent knight and the most honourable and worthy man I have ever met. He is without deceit, wickedness or treachery and he shall achieve much. Now most courteous and gentle knight, give me back the sword.'

'No!' said Balin, who had been examining it and found it greatly to his liking. 'I shall keep this sword unless it is taken from me by force.'

'You are not wise to keep it from me,' said the lady, 'for with that sword you will slay your best friend and the man you love above all others. I tell you, the sword will bring about your destruction!'

'I shall accept whatever fate God sends me,' said Balin, 'but I swear I shall not return the sword to you.'

'Then you will soon regret it,' the lady told him. 'I ask for the sword more for your sake than for mine and I am truly sorry for you – you plainly do not believe that it will destroy you, but I speak the truth when I warn you of tragedy.' With that she left the court with a great show of grief.

After the lady had departed, Balin sent for his horse and armour and went to take his leave of the king. 'Alas! I have done you a great injustice,' said King Arthur with genuine regret, 'yet do not part from this fellowship so readily. I know you must be angry, but do not blame me entirely, for I was misinformed against you. I never dreamt that you were a knight of such valour and honour. If you will stay here at Camelot I swear that you shall be rewarded.'

'Your Majesty's kindness is beyond praise, and I thank you for it,' said Balin. 'But now I must leave and I hope that I may do so with your blessing.'

'You have it, fair knight,' the king replied, 'although I am indeed sorry to see you go, and beg you not to stay away too long. You will always be most welcome here and I promise to make amends for the wrong I have done you.'

'God thank you,' said Balin, and prepared to depart.

At that moment, a beautifully dressed lady arrived at King Arthur's court on horseback; it was the Lady of the Lake, come to ask the king for the gift he had promised her. 'Indeed, I did promise you a gift,' the king agreed, 'but I forgot to ask you the name of the sword you gave me.'

'The name of the sword is Excalibur,' said the Lady of the Lake, 'which is to say "Cut Steel".'

'It is well named,' the king replied. 'Ask of me whatever you wish, and if it is within my power, you shall have it.'

'I ask for the head of that knight who won the sword from the lady,' said the Lady of the Lake, 'or else the head of the lady herself. Either will do, but to have both would be better, for he killed my brother, who was a good and true knight, and she was the cause of my father's death.'

'I can grant you neither of their heads!' said King Arthur, aghast. 'In truth, my honour forbids it. But ask whatever else you desire and you shall have it.'

'I ask for nothing else,' said the lady.

As he was about to ride away from King Arthur's court, Balin saw the Lady of the Lake. She had brought about his mother's death and so he had been seeking her for several years. When he was told that she had asked King Arthur for his head, Balin went to her straight away in a terrible rage. 'May you be cursed!' he cried. 'You would have my head? Very well – you shall lose yours!' and, with one quick stroke of his sword, he smote her head from her shoulders in front of the king.

'Alas! For shame!' said King Arthur, horrified. 'Why have you done this? You have disgraced me and my court. This was a lady to whom I was greatly indebted, and upon entering this court she was under my protection. I shall never forgive you for such a violation!'

'My lord, I am deeply grieved to have so displeased you,' said Balin unhappily. 'But I swear that she was the most wicked lady alive, for by her witchcraft and enchantment she destroyed many good knights – and it was her treachery that caused my own mother to be burnt.'

'No matter what reason you had, you should not have done this in my presence,' said the king. 'And I swear you shall repent it, for I have never received such an insult in my court before. Therefore withdraw from us immediately.'

So Balin took up the lady's head and left King Arthur's court. At his lodging he was met by his squire, to whom he gave the severed head. 'Take this to my friends in Northumberland,' he said, 'and tell them that my greatest foe is now dead. Tell them also that I am freed from prison and explain how I succeeded in drawing the sword.'

'Yet I fear you are in the wrong for so offending the king,' the squire reminded him.

'As for that,' said Balin, 'I shall ride with all speed to find King Rience of North Wales and destroy him, or die in the attempt. If I am fortunate enough to succeed, King Arthur will surely forgive me.'

'Where shall I meet you?' asked the squire.

'At King Arthur's court,' Balin replied.

So Balin and his squire rode off in their separate directions, while at Camelot King Arthur and his knights mourned the death of the Lady of the Lake and the king arranged a splendid burial for her.

One of King Arthur's knights – the son of a king of Ireland – was called Lanceor; he was proud and boastful and considered himself to be the finest knight at court. He was reluctant to admit that any other knight could be more courageous or skilful than himself. Therefore he felt considerable animosity towards Balin for having achieved the sword, and asked King Arthur if he could ride after him to avenge the Lady of the Lake.

'Do your best,' the king replied. 'I am deeply angry with Balin and certainly wish him to redeem the wrong he has done.'

So Lanceor armed himself, mounted his horse, took up his lance and shield and rode after Balin le Savage as fast as he could. Before long, on a mountain ascent, he caught sight of Balin and shouted to him at the top of his voice, 'Stay, knight! I say you shall stay whether you wish to or not! And your shield will be no protection against me, I promise you.'

'Perhaps you would have done better to have remained at home,' said Balin, reining in his horse and looking at his pompous challenger. 'For many a man who boasts of defeating his opponent finds he is defeated himself. What court do you come from?'

'I am from the court of King Arthur,' replied the Irish knight, 'and I have come to avenge the grievous wrong you have done the king and his court.'

'Then I must accept your challenge,' Balin conceded, 'for it distresses me greatly that I have grieved King Arthur or any of his court. But in truth you have little need to quarrel with me,

for the lady I killed had done me great harm, else I should have
been as loath as any knight to have killed a lady.'
'Make ready and prepare to fight with me,' said Lanceor. 'Only
one of us shall remain alive here!'

The two knights fixed their spears into their rests and rode at
each other as fast as their horses would gallop. The Irish knight
smote Balin so fiercely upon his shield that it shattered. Then
Balin struck Lanceor through his own shield, destroying his coat
of mail and piercing his body. Lanceor was thrown from his
mount and Balin turned his own horse sharply and drew his
sword, not realising that he had already killed his opponent.

As Balin looked at the dead knight lying on the ground, a lady
on a palfrey rode up at great speed. When she saw Lanceor lying
there, she dismounted and rushed towards his body, sobbing
loudly. 'Oh, cruel knight!' she cried to Balin, 'you have slain two
bodies in one heart and two hearts in one body!' and she took
the dead knight's sword and fell in a faint beside him.

When she regained her senses she wept so piteously that Balin
was filled with compassion for her. He attempted to take the
sword from her hand but she gripped it so tightly that he could
not remove it without hurting her. Suddenly, she placed the
pummel of the sword on the ground and threw herself hard upon
the point, stabbing herself through the heart. When Balin saw
what she had done he felt saddened and ashamed. 'Alas!' he said,
'I bitterly regret that so fair a maid should kill herself because
I have slain this knight. This was true love!'

He was so moved by pity that he could no longer bear to look
upon the dead lovers, and turned his horse instead towards a
forest. As he did so, another knight came riding towards him,
and to his great delight he saw that it was his brother, Balan.
When the two knights met they put up their helmets and
embraced each other, weeping tears of joy.

'Brother, I little expected to meet with you at a scene such as
this,' said Balan, indicating the dead knight and his lady. 'But I
am pleased that you have been freed from your unjust
imprisonment. I was told by a man at the Castle of Four Stones

that you were released, and that he had seen you in the court of King Arthur. Therefore I rode with all haste to find you.'
Balin then told his brother of his adventure with the sword and the death of the Lady of the Lake, and how King Arthur was displeased with him. 'So he sent this knight after me, who now lies dead. But the death of the maiden sorely distresses me.'

'It distresses me too,' Balan admitted, 'but you must accept whatever adventure God has ordained for you.'

'It grieves me very much that King Arthur is displeased with me,' said Balin, 'and I will willingly risk my life to win his love. King Rience is at present besieging Castle Terrabil, so I shall ride there at speed and use all my skills to defeat him.'

'It is right that you should do so,' Balan agreed, 'and I will ride with you and put my life at risk with yours, as a good brother should.'

'We shall do well together,' said Balin. 'Come, let us start out on our quest immediately.'

Their departure was delayed, however, by the appearance of a dwarf on horseback, who rode up to them at great speed. When he saw the dead bodies he wailed and pulled at his hair. 'Which of you knights has done this?' he asked.

Balin admitted that he was responsible for the deaths. 'The knight I killed in self-defence,' he said, 'for he came after me to kill me. The lady killed herself for love of the knight, and that I regret most deeply.'

'You have done yourself no favours here!' said the dwarf. 'The dead knight was one of the most valiant that ever lived. Believe me, Balin, the kin of this knight will pursue you until they kill you.'

'As for that,' said Balin, 'I have no great fear, but I am deeply sorry to have further displeased King Arthur by killing this knight.'

While they were talking, King Mark of Cornwall chanced to ride that way. On seeing the bodies and learning how the knight and his lady had died, he expressed great sorrow and vowed that he would find a rich tomb to cover them. Then he asked Balin his name.

Balan answered for his brother. 'Sir,' he said, 'you will see that he carries two swords, and that is what you may call him: the Knight with the Two Swords.'

When King Mark and the dwarf had departed there was yet another delay for Merlin appeared.

'Ah, Balin!' he said reproachfully, 'you have done yourself much damage by not preventing this lady from killing herself. You could have saved her had you tried.'

'By my faith I could not!' said Balin. 'She fell upon the sword too suddenly.'

'It grieves me,' said Merlin. 'Because of the death of that lady, you will strike the most dolorous (grievous) stroke that any knight has ever struck, for you shall wound the truest and most honourable man alive. Through that stroke three kingdoms shall be brought into great poverty, misery and wretchedness for twelve years, and for many years the knight you strike shall not be healed of his wound.'

'No!' cried Balin in horror, 'it cannot be so! If I thought that what you say is true – that I could indeed do anything so terrible – I swear I would kill myself first!'

Merlin made no reply to this, for he had vanished as suddenly as he had appeared, and the two brothers at last set out on their quest. They had not journeyed far before they were stopped by a strange man at the wayside. 'Where are you riding to?' the stranger asked.

'I think we have little reason to tell you,' said Balin. 'But what is your name?'

'I shall not tell you at this time,' said the stranger.

'It is a sure sign that you are not an honest man, if you will not give us your name,' said Balan.

'Be that as it may,' replied the stranger. 'I can tell you why you are riding this way – you hope to meet with King Rience. But it will do you no good unless you have my counsel.'

'I know you now!' said Balin. 'You are Merlin and we shall be guided by your counsel.'

It was indeed Merlin, who now appeared as himself. 'Come with me then,' he said 'and you shall have great honour.' Balin and his brother Balan went with the magician into a wood, where he told them to rest among some leaves by the highway. They unbridled their horses and put them to grass, and then lay down under the foliage until it was almost midnight, at which time Merlin roused them.

'Make yourselves ready,' he whispered, 'for the king is coming. He has ridden away from his army by night with three score of his best knights and their horses. Twenty of them have ridden on ahead to warn the Lady de Vance that he is coming, for he is to lie with her tonight.'

'Which is the king?' Balin asked.

'You shall see him directly,' Merlin replied, 'for he comes now.'

The two brothers silently mounted their horses and rode out to meet the king. They wounded him and battled with his knights. Having taken them by surprise – with Merlin's guidance – they were able to kill more than forty of them and the rest fled. They then returned to King Rience and would have killed him too, had he not yielded to them and begged for mercy.

'Brave and worthy knights, do not slay me!' pleaded King Rience. 'For by my life you may win much, and by my death very little.'

The brothers agreed that he spoke the truth, and so they put him on a horse-litter. Meanwhile, Merlin had vanished from the scene, and now appeared to King Arthur at Camelot to tell him how his enemy had been vanquished.

'By whom?' King Arthur enquired.

'By two knights who most willingly serve you,' said Merlin. 'And tomorrow you shall know who they are.'

Soon the Knight with the Two Swords and his brother, Balan, arrived at Camelot, bringing with them King Rience of North Wales and delivering him into the charge of the porters at King Arthur's castle. The two brothers then departed as dawn was breaking.

'Sir, you are welcome,' said King Arthur courteously, when the captured King of North Wales was brought before him. 'By what adventure have you come here?'

'Sir,' replied King Rience, 'by a very hard adventure!'

'Who defeated you?'

'Sir, the Knight with the Two Swords and his brother; two knights of marvellous and unusual skill.'

King Arthur shook his head. 'I do not know them,' he said.

Then Merlin stepped forward. 'I shall tell you who they are,' he said. 'It is Balin, sir, who drew out the sword from the damsel's girdle, and with him his brother Balan who is a knight of great skill and honour. It is a shame that such a worthy knight is soon to die.'

'Alas,' said King Arthur, 'if what you say is true then it is indeed a pity, for I owe much to that knight. I have not deserved that he should do me such kindness.'

'He shall do much more for you, my lord,' Merlin promised, 'and you shall know of it very soon.'

The Dolorous Stroke

 ing Arthur was exhausted and in need of rest after defeating Nero, King Rience's brother, in battle. Although Nero had had the larger army, Arthur and his knights had triumphed and had killed Nero and most of his men.

The Knight with the Two Swords and his brother, Balan, fought for King Arthur and displayed such death-dealing skill that those who saw them thought they must either be angels sent from heaven or devils sent from hell. The king himself declared that they were the most marvellous knights he had ever seen on the battlefield.

Merlin deliberately detained King Lot of the Orkneys, for he would have gone to Nero's aid and then Arthur would certainly have been defeated. As it was, Lot battled with King Arthur's knights after Nero was killed, and acquitted himself very well, for he was a brave knight who had once fought on the side of King Arthur. King Lot was finally killed by King Pellinore, who was known as the King with the Strange Beast – a name given to him because he hunted the Questing Beast, which was so oddly formed from parts of various creatures.

Twelve kings on the side of Nero and Lot were killed in the battle, and they were all buried in the church of St Stevens at Camelot. King Arthur had a special tomb made for his brother-in-law, King Lot, and as a mark of respect he had it placed on its own, set apart from the other tombs.

Now the battles were over and King Arthur could afford to rest, so he ordered his pavilion to be pitched in a meadow and lay down on a pallet to sleep. Sleep evaded him, however, and when he was disturbed by the sound of a horse's hooves close to his pavilion, he looked out to see a knight riding by, moaning sadly to himself.

'Stay a moment, sir,' said King Arthur, 'and tell me why you are so sorrowful.'

'You can do little to help me,' the knight replied, and rode on towards the castle of Meliot, still moaning woefully.

Shortly after this, Balin le Savage rode into the meadow, and when he saw King Arthur at his pavilion he dismounted and greeted him with due respect.

'Ah, Balin, you are most welcome!' said King Arthur. 'A knight just rode past here in deep distress, but he would not give me the reason. I ask you, in courtesy, to bring that knight to me, whether he will come willingly or not.'

'I shall indeed, my lord,' said Balin, 'and if he resists I shall bring him by force.'

So Balin rode after the mournful knight at great speed, and found him in a forest with a lady. 'Sir, knight,' said Balin, 'you must come with me to King Arthur and tell him the cause of your sorrow.'

'I will not,' the knight replied, 'for it will do me much harm and bring no honour to you.'

'Sir, I beg you to accompany me,' said Balin. 'For if you won't I must fight with you and take you by force, and I do not wish to do that.'

'Will you protect me if I come with you?' asked the knight.

'Indeed, with my life,' Balin assured him.

So the knight left his lady and rode with Balin towards King Arthur's pavilion. They had not long left the forest when a spear hit the mournful knight, fatally wounding him. Balin was amazed, for he had seen no one approach.

'Alas!' gasped the wounded knight, 'I am slain while under your protection by a treacherous knight called Garlon. Take my horse, for it is faster than yours, ride to the lady and ask her to lead you on the quest that was mine. Avenge my death when you can.'

'That I shall do without fail,' said Balin. 'I swear it on my knighthood.' He then left the knight and rode to King Arthur. The king arranged for the knight to be richly buried, and the lady took the shaft of the spear that had killed him and carried it with her always.

It was now Balin who moaned sorrowfully to himself as he and the lady rode back into the forest. There they met a knight who had been hunting and he asked Balin the cause of his great sorrow. 'I do not wish to tell you,' Balin replied.

'Well,' said the knight, 'if I was armed as you are, I should fight you to learn the reason.'

'There is no need for fighting,' said Balin, 'for I am not afraid to tell you,' and he explained to the knight what had happened to make him sorrowful.

'Is that all?' said the knight. 'Then I shall ride with you, and I swear never to leave your side while my breath lasts.'

Balin and the lady went with the knight to his lodging and waited while he armed himself. Then he rejoined them and all three set off on their quest. But as they rode past a hermitage near a churchyard, the knight was struck through the body with a spear, although neither Balin nor the lady had seen anyone approach.

'Alas!' cried the knight, mortally wounded, 'I am killed by that treacherous knight who rides invisible!'

'This is not the first wrong he has done me,' said Balin, wretched with grief.

He and the hermit buried the knight with care and placed a fine stone over his grave. Then Balin and the lady rode on together until they came to a castle. Balin went through the gate first, whereupon the portcullis came down behind him and the lady was left on the other side of it. A number of men quickly surrounded her as if they would kill her, and Balin was enraged because the lowered portcullis prevented him going to her assistance.

He leapt on to the castle wall and was able to jump into the ditch and land, unhurt, on the same side of the portcullis as the lady and her assailants. He drew his sword immediately to fight with the men, but they refused to fight and told him that they were only following the custom of the castle.

'The lady of this castle has been sick for many years,' said one of the men, who was a retainer at the castle, 'and the only thing that will cure her is a silver dish filled with the blood of a pure maiden of royal birth. Therefore, it is the custom here that no lady may pass this way unless she gives a silver dishful of her blood.'

'Well,' said Balin, 'this lady may give of her blood if she chooses to do so but she shall not lose her life as long as I have mine!'

The damsel agreed to give her blood to help the unfortunate lady and bravely held out her arm so that Balin could cut it over the silver dish. When the dish was filled, the retainer took it to the lady of the castle and Balin bound the damsel's arm. Her blood did not help the ailing lady, but she and Balin were invited to rest in the castle overnight and were given generous refreshment and cheerful hospitality.

The following morning, Balin and the damsel set out together, she leading the way as had been promised. For four days they journeyed without further adventure, and on the fourth night good fortune brought them to the house of a rich gentleman who was delighted to have their company. As they were sitting at supper, Balin heard someone in a nearby room complaining loudly.

'What noise is that?' he asked their host.

'I will tell you,' the gentleman replied. 'I was jousting recently and I fought with a knight who is the brother of King Pellam of Listenise. Twice I managed to strike him down. Then he swore to take revenge on the person who is most dear to me. He wounded my son – you can hear him now, crying out in pain – and the boy cannot be healed until I have that same knight's blood. But he rides invisible and I do not know his name.'

'I know that knight!' said Balin. 'His name is Garlon and he has slain two of my knights in the same manner. I tell you, I would rather fight with that knight for the terrible wrong he has done me than own all the gold in this kingdom!'

'Well,' said his host, 'you may have your chance, for you have your lady with you.' Balin did not understand, so his host went on to explain. 'King Pellam has made it known throughout the land that he will be giving a great feast within twenty days, but no knight may attend unless he is accompanied by his wife or lady for whom he will do battle. You would be able to go to the feast and there you will find your enemy and mine.'

'I promise you,' said Balin, 'that you shall have some of his blood to heal your son.'

'Then we shall set out tomorrow morning,' replied the host, much gratified by Balin's pledge.

The following morning the three of them started on their journey to King Pellam's court. They rode for many days before they arrived at the king's castle, where the feasting had just commenced. They dismounted and stabled their horses, but Balin's host was not allowed to enter the castle because he had no lady. Balin, however, was warmly received and taken to a room where he could disarm and put on comfortable robes that were brought to him. He was then asked to leave his swords behind. 'No,' he said firmly, 'that I will not do, for it is the custom

of my country that a knight always has his weapon with him.
I must conform to that custom or I regret that I must leave as I
came.' They agreed to let him wear one of his swords and he
went into the castle, where he was seated among some of the
most noble knights with his lady beside him.

When the feasting was under way, Balin turned to one of his
fellow guests. 'Is there not a knight in this court named Garlon?'
he asked.

'Over there,' his companion replied. 'He is the one with the
black face. He is the most marvellous knight living. He kills
many good knights because he rides invisible.'

'Ah!' said Balin, 'so that is he!' He looked at the knight with the
black face and pondered for some time. 'If I kill him here I shall
not escape,' he thought, 'but if I leave him now, perhaps I shall
never have such an opportunity again – and if he continues to
live, he will do much damage.'

Garlon saw Balin looking at him speculatively and crossed the
floor to him, striking him across the face with the back of his
hand. 'Knight, why do you stare at me like that?' he demanded.
'For shame, eat your meat and do what you came to do.'

'You speak the truth!' said Balin. 'This is not the first wrong you
have done me and so I shall do what I came to do.' With that he
rose to his feet, drew his sword and sliced Garlon's head from his
body at the shoulders.

'Give me the spear with which he killed your knight,' he said to
the lady. She gave Balin the shaft of the spear she always carried
with her, and he struck Garlon with it through his body. 'With
that spear shaft you killed a noble knight. Now it sticks in your
own body,' said Balin. Then he called to the gentleman who had
been his host to come and fetch enough of Garlon's blood to heal
his son.

Straight away, all the knights rose from the table to set upon
Balin, and King Pellam himself rose up in great anger. 'Knight,

why have you killed my brother?' he cried. 'You shall die for this before you depart.'

'Then kill me yourself!' Balin retorted.

'I shall!' said King Pellam. 'No man but I shall avenge the death of my brother.' He seized a great log from beside the burning fire and struck at Balin fiercely, breaking his sword in two. Weaponless, Balin ran into another room to seek something with which to defend himself. He found nothing, so ran desperately from chamber to chamber in search of a weapon, and always King Pellam was close behind him.

At last he entered a splendidly furnished room in which someone lay in a bed covered with the richest cloth of gold. Nearby stood a table of gold supported by legs of pure silver, and on the table was a most magnificent spear, wrought in the finest fashion imaginable.

Balin took up the spear and, turning to King Pellam, struck him with it. The king fell in a swoon, deeply wounded, and as he did so the castle began to break up. Roof and wall broke apart and crashed to the ground, and Balin fell with them, unable to move any part of his body. Most of the other people in the castle were killed immediately, and Balin and King Pellam lay helpless for three whole days.

Then Merlin arrived. He lifted Balin to his feet and found him a good horse, for his own horse was dead, and told him to leave that country as quickly as possible.

'Sir, I must find my lady,' said Balin.

'Look,' said Merlin, pointing, 'there she lies, dead!'

Merlin and Balin parted company when they rode away from King Pellam's ruined castle. 'We shall not meet again in this world,' said the magician.

Balin rode through the fair countries and cities and found the people lying dead on every side. Those who were left alive called out to him as he passed: 'Ah, Balin! What you have done has caused terrible damage in these countries. Because of the dolorous stroke you gave to King Pellam, these three countries are destroyed! Have no doubt that vengeance will fall upon you in the end!'

King Pellam lay deeply wounded for many years. He could not be cured until Sir Galahad healed him in his quest for the Holy Grail, for Balin had struck the dolorous stroke just as Merlin had prophesied. The room where he found the spear held a vessel containing some of the blood of Jesus Christ, which Joseph of Arimathea had brought to the land. It was Joseph himself – close kin to King Pellam – who lay in the bed. The spear with which Balin had wounded the king was none other than that with which Longeus (Longinus), the Roman soldier, had pierced the side of Christ at the crucifixion. So it came about that the dolorous stroke wounded King Pellam and brought great suffering and sorrow to the land.

Balin was filled with misery as he rode through the stricken countries, but once he had left them behind, his spirits began to rise and he was ready for adventure once more. After riding on for eight days he came to a delightful forest in a valley. There he saw a tower, near to which a very large horse was tethered to a tree. Beside the horse sat a handsome knight who was moaning tragically, although to Balin's eye he was such a well-favoured young man that he should have had little to moan about!

'God save you, why are you so sad?' Balin asked him. 'Tell me, and if it is within my power, I shall rid you of your sadness.'

'Sir knight,' said the other, 'you do me a disservice, for my thoughts were merry ones and now you have caused me to suffer again.'

In deference to the young knight's feelings, Balin moved away from him and examined his fine war horse. Then he heard the knight say: 'Ah, fair lady, why have you broken your word? You promised to meet me here by noon. Now I curse you for giving me this sword, for I shall kill myself with it!' And he pulled the sword from its sheath. Balin immediately sprang to his side and took him by the hand. 'Let go of my hand,' said the knight, 'or I shall kill you.'

'There is no need for that,' said Balin, 'for I promise I will help you to get your lady if you will tell me where she is.'

'What is your name?' said the knight.

'My name is Balin le Savage.'

'Ah, sir, I have heard much of you. You are the Knight with the Two Swords and the most valiant man alive.'

'What is your name?' asked Balin.

'My name is Garnish of the Mount and I am a poor man's son, but because of my courage and skill Duke Hermel has made me a knight and given me lands of my own. His daughter is the lady I love – and whom I thought loved me.'

'How far away is the duke's castle?'

'No more than five miles.'

'Then we shall ride there at once to find your lady,' said Balin.

The two knights mounted their horses and rode at a good speed until they reached a handsome, well-built castle with a wide ditch. 'I will go inside and look for her,' said Balin. He went into the castle and searched every room, but there was no sign of the lady. Then he came across a pretty little garden behind the castle and there he saw her asleep. She lay upon a green silk quilt and she was clasped in the arms of a sleeping knight, their two heads resting on a pillow of herbs and grass. Balin could see that she was indeed a fair lady, but the knight looked more unwholesome than any he had ever seen.

He hurried back to Garnish of the Mount and told him that he had found his lady sleeping fast and that he would take him to where she slept. So he led him through the castle to the little garden, and when the young knight saw his lady sleeping in the arms of her foul lover he was so distraught that blood issued from his nose and mouth, and he pulled out his sword and cut off the heads of both the lady and the sleeping knight. Then he wept bitterly and without restraint.

'Oh, Balin!' he cried, 'what untold misery you have brought upon me! If you had not shown me that sight I should have been spared my terrible sorrow.'

'I did it with the best intention,' said Balin. 'In showing you her falsehood I thought you would realise she was unworthy of your love. God knows, I only did what I should want you to do for me.'

'Alas!' said the stricken knight, 'now my sorrow is too great to bear, for I have destroyed what I loved most in all the world.'

Before Balin could prevent it, he ran upon his own sword up to the hilt, killing himself instantly. Balin was distressed to see this, but he was also aware that anyone arriving on the scene could be forgiven for thinking that he had slain all three of them. So he left quickly and rode away from the castle.

After riding for three days he came to a cross upon which, in letters of gold, were written the words:

IT IS NOT FOR A KNIGHT ALONE TO RIDE TOWARDS THIS CASTLE.

As he paused to ponder the message, an old man with white hair came towards him. 'Balin le Savage,' he said, 'you pass your bounds by coming this way. Turn back now and it will be to your advantage.' Whereupon the old man disappeared.

Then Balin heard a horn blow, as if it heralded the death of a beast. 'That blast is blown for me,' he thought, 'for I am the prize and yet I am not dead!'

Within a matter of minutes he saw a crowd of about a hundred ladies and many knights. They surrounded him, smiling pleasantly and making him welcome. They led him to the castle where he dismounted and was taken inside. Here there was dancing and music and all manner of cheerful celebrations. Then the chief lady of the castle addressed him.

'Knight with the Two Swords, you must prepare yourself to joust with a knight near here who keeps an island. No man can pass this way unless he jousts.'

'That is an unhappy custom,' said Balin, 'for a knight not to be allowed to pass this way unless he jousts!'

'You will only have to do battle with one knight,' the lady assured him.

'Well,' said Balin, 'since I have to, I am ready to do so. But travelling men are often tired and so are their horses. My own horse is weary – but my heart is not. I am ready to fight, even if I am to be killed.'

'Sir,' said a knight, 'I do not think your shield is good enough and I will lend you a larger one. Take it, I pray you.' So Balin took the unmarked shield and left his own behind, and he and his horse were taken across to the island in a large boat. When they had landed on the island he met a lady.

'O sir knight, Balin, why have you left your shield behind?' she asked. 'Alas! You have put yourself in great danger, for you would have been known by your shield. It is such a pity, for there is not a knight living who can match you for skill and courage.'

'I regret that I ever came to this country,' Balin admitted. 'But if I turn back now I shall be dishonoured, so I must take whatever adventure befalls me. And whether it be life or death, I accept it.'

He examined his armour, and being satisfied that all was in order, crossed himself and mounted his horse. Then, out of the castle on the island, rode a knight dressed all in red with his horse in trappings of the same colour. Setting their spears, the two knights rode towards each other at a tremendous pace, and came together with such force that both men and horses were brought to the ground, where the two knights lay in a faint.

The knight in red rose to his feet first, for Balin was travel-weary and bruised by his falling horse. The red knight drew his sword and Balin arose and went towards him, but the other was faster, striking Balin through his shield and splitting his helmet. Balin struck back, almost felling the red knight – and so they fought together until their strength was all but spent.

Balin looked up at the castle and saw a great many ladies in the tower, watching the combat. The two knights went into battle again, wounding each other pitilessly. They paused from time to time to draw breath and then returned to the fray with such ferocity that, wherever they fought, the ground was red with their blood. By now they both had no less than seven massive wounds – each of which might well have been the death of an ordinary man.

Another pause, and the ladies sighed and feared that the fighting was over. Then Balin and the red knight went into battle again with such astonishing force that it was a fearful thing to hear tell of that fight afterwards. Their coats of mail were torn apart and they were left naked.

At last the red knight faltered, drew apart a little and lay down on the ground. 'What knight are you?' Balin gasped. 'Until now I have never found a knight that matched me.'

'My name is Balan,' the red knight replied weakly, 'and I am brother to the good knight Balin.'

'Alas!' said Balin, 'that I should ever see this day!' and he fell back in a swoon.

His younger brother, Balan, crawled to him on all fours and lifted his helmet, but could not recognise his face for it was so cut and bloody. When Balin regained consciousness he cried, 'O my brother, Balan! You have slain me and I have slain you; the whole world shall speak of this!'

'Alas!' said Balan, 'that through misfortune I did not know you! Because you had another shield, I took you for another knight.'

'It was an unlucky kindness, offered by a knight at the castle, that caused me to leave my shield behind – and in doing so brought about the death of both of us. If I could live I would destroy that castle for its ill custom.'

'It would be a charitable act,' said Balan, 'for I have not been able to leave since I came here and killed the knight who kept this island. Neither could you have departed, my brother, had you killed me and continued to live yourself.'

Then the lady of the castle came to them, with four knights, six ladies and six yeomen attendant upon them, and she heard how the brothers had fought and slain each other unwittingly. 'We came from the same mother's womb,' they told her, 'and so we shall lie together in one grave.'

Balan begged the lady that out of her gratitude for his faithful service she would bury them together where their battle had been fought. And she, weeping, agreed that this should be done.

'Now will you send for a priest so that we may receive the sacrament?'

'Yes,' said the lady, 'that shall be done also,' and she sent for a priest who performed the last rites.

'When we are buried in one tomb,' said Balin, 'and it is written on our tomb how two brothers killed each other, no good man shall ever see it without praying for our souls.' Whereupon all the ladies wept for pity.

Balan died very quickly but his brother, Balin, did not die until the following night. So they were buried together, and the lady had it written on their tomb how Balan was slain by his brother's hand, but she did not know Balin's name.

The next morning Merlin arrived, and wrote on the tomb in letters of gold:

HERE LIETH BALIN LE SAVAGE, THAT WAS THE KNIGHT WITH THE TWO SWORDS, AND HE THAT STRUCK THE DOLOROUS STROKE

The Round Table

erlin was King Arthur's counsellor and advised him on almost every subject. Not long after the death of Balin and Balan, Arthur told the magician that his barons were urging him to take a wife.

'It would be a good idea,' Merlin agreed. 'A man of your status should not be without a wife. Tell me, is there one lady whom you love better than any other?'

'Yes,' said Arthur, 'I am in love with Guinevere, the daughter of King Leodegrance of Cameliard. She is the sweetest and most beautiful lady alive.'

'She is fair enough,' Merlin admitted, 'but she will bring you unhappiness, for Lancelot will love her and she will return his love.' Yet even as he spoke, Merlin knew that if a man sets his heart on a certain lady there is no turning him aside.

Instead of arguing further he agreed to act as an intermediary, first making discreet enquiries about Guinevere herself, and then going to her father and telling him of King Arthur's desire to marry her. King Leodegrance was delighted.

'These are the best tidings I ever had!' he said. 'To think that so worthy and powerful a king should marry my daughter! I would happily give him gifts of lands but he has many of his own, so I shall send him something that will please him much more: I shall give him the Table Round that King Uther Pendragon gave to me. It will seat one hundred and fifty knights when full, and I can send a hundred good knights of my own, but I lack the other fifty for I have lost so many in battle.'

King Leodegrance delivered his daughter Guinevere to Merlin, with the Round Table and the hundred knights, and they travelled in great style by land and water and rested that night in the city of London. When Arthur heard that Guinevere was coming to him, he was overjoyed. 'Nothing could make me happier than to receive this fair lady to be my wife,' he said, 'for I have loved her for a long time. And the gift of the knights with the Round Table pleases me more than great riches.'

He ordered the wedding and coronation to take place as soon as possible, in the best and most noble manner that could be arranged. Then he addressed his magician.

'Merlin, go and search until you have found me fifty of the finest and most honourable knights in the land.'

Merlin found twenty-eight good knights, but he could find no more. Then the Archbishop of Canterbury was sent for, to bless the sieges (seats) of Arthur's Round Table. After the blessing, the knights rose to pay homage to their king and then left. When they had left, Merlin discovered that all but two of the sieges bore the name of a knight, written boldly in letters of gold.

Young Gawain, the son of Lot and Margawse, longed to occupy one of the vacant sieges and begged King Arthur to make him a knight on the day of his marriage to Guinevere. 'So I shall, most willingly,' the king replied, 'and you shall be held in the highest esteem, because you are my nephew and my sister's son.'

There now remained but one empty siege and Merlin named it the 'Siege Perilous' or 'Seat of Danger'. In the fullness of time it would come to be occupied by Galahad, son of Sir Lancelot and the holiest of all the Knights of the Round Table.

Culhwch and Olwen

From *The Mabinogion*

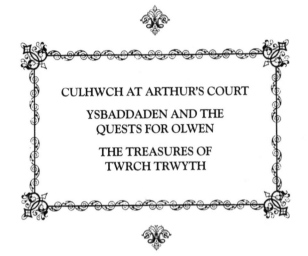

CULHWCH AT ARTHUR'S COURT

YSBADDADEN AND THE
QUESTS FOR OLWEN

THE TREASURES OF
TWRCH TRWYTH

GWRHYR: …whose is the fort?
SHEPHERD: Throughout the world it is known
that this is the fort of Ysbaddaden Chief
Giant… who are you?
GWRHYR: Messengers of Arthur… to seek Olwen.
SHEPHERD: Whew, men! God protect you! For all
the world do not that. Never a one has come
to make that request that went away with
his life.

From The Four Independent Native Tales

ulhwch, son of Cilydd the king, was a fine youth and first cousin to Arthur. One day Culhwch's step-mother said to him, 'It is time for you to take a wife, son, and I have a daughter who is a fitting match for any nobleman in the world.'

'But I am not yet old enough to take a wife,' the boy replied hastily.

'Then I swear upon you an impossible destiny!' cried the queen, angered to think that her own daughter had been spurned. 'You shall never have any woman for wife until you win Olwen, daughter of Ysbaddaden Chief Giant.'

At the mention of the giant's daughter, Culhwch flushed deeply, and love for Olwen flooded every limb of his body although he had never met her. 'Why, son, what ails you?' asked his father, seeing the boy's heightened colour.

'My step-mother has sworn on me that I shall never win a wife until I win Olwen, daughter of Ysbaddaden Chief Giant,' said Culhwch.

'Well, son, it should be easy for you to achieve that,' the king replied. 'Arthur is your first cousin. Go to him and ask him to trim your hair and then, as a gift, ask him for that which your step-mother has sworn on you.'

So Culhwch put on a mantle of richest purple and rode off on a shell-hoofed steed, seated on a saddle of gold. So light and sure-footed was this horse that not a hair stirred on Culhwch's head as he cantered to Arthur's court. When he reached the gate, he saw one man at the entrance and he asked him if there was a porter.

'There is,' replied the man, who was called Glewlwyd Mighty-grasp, 'I am porter to Arthur every first day of January, but I have four deputies for every day of the year other than that. One of those deputies is none other than Penpingion, who goes upon his head to save his feet, not heavenwards or earthwards, but like a rolling stone on the court floor.'

'Open the gate,' said Culhwch impatiently.

'I will not,' replied Glewlwyd, 'for knife has gone into meat and drink into horn and the company is assembled in Arthur's court. Tomorrow, when the gate is opened for guests, you shall be the first to enter and you may sit wherever you will, from the upper to the lower end of Arthur's hall.'

'If you do not open the gate now, I shall bring dishonour upon your lord and ill report upon you,' said Culhwch. 'And I shall raise three shouts at the entrance to this gate that will be heard on the top of Pengwaedd in Cornwall, in the depths of Dinsel in the north, and in Esgeir Oerfel in Ireland.'

'Shout as much as you like,' said Glewlwyd Mighty-grasp, 'but I shall not let you in until I have spoken with Arthur.'

'Have you news from the gate?' asked Arthur, when Glewlwyd appeared in the hall.

'I have,' Glewlwyd replied. 'I have shared many adventures with you. I was with you when you killed Mil the Black, son of Dugum; I was there when you conquered Greece; and I was there in Anoeth and in Caer Nefenhyr Nine-teeth. We saw many a kingly man in those places but I never saw a man so comely as the one who now stands at the gate.'

'You came in walking but you shall go out running,' said Arthur sternly, 'for it is a shameful thing to leave a man such as you describe in the wind and rain.'

Glewlwyd left in haste and Arthur addressed his warriors. 'Fetch golden drinking horns and hot peppered chops, so that there is ample meat and drink for our fair guest.'

'If you listened to my counsel,' said Cei, one of the warriors, 'the laws of court would not be broken for his sake.'

'Not so, fair Cei!' Arthur replied. 'We are noble men only so long as we are called upon to help others, and the greater our generosity, the greater our nobility and glory.'

Meanwhile, Glewlwyd hurried back to the gate and opened it for Culhwch, who ignored the horse-block placed so that visitors could dismount before entering, and rode his horse into Arthur's hall. From his saddle he greeted the king with great courtesy.

'Hail, sovereign prince of this island! May this greeting be no less to the lower part of your house than to the upper. May it be equally to your noblemen and to their attendants and to the leaders of your armies. May there be none without his share of it. And even as I give you this greeting, may your grace and glory be esteemed in this island.'

'So be it, chieftain! Greetings to you too,' said Arthur warmly. 'Sit between two of my warriors and you shall be treated in the most royal manner for as long as you remain here. There shall be song and wine and whatever else you may wish.'

'I have not come here for meat and drink,' said the boy. 'But if I obtain my boon (favour) I will praise your hospitality and repay it. If I do not obtain it I shall take your honour with me to the farthest corners of the world.'

'Whether you stay here or not, you shall have any boon you wish,' said Arthur. 'Now, name what you will.'

'First,' said Culhwch, 'I would have my hair trimmed.'

'So you shall,' the king replied and, taking up a golden comb and shears with loops of silver, he combed the boy's head. 'I feel a great tenderness towards you. I know you must be of my blood. Tell me who you are.'

'I am Culhwch, son of Cilydd. Goleuddydd was my mother.'

'Then it is true,' said Arthur. 'You are my first cousin. Name what you will and you shall have it, whatever it is.'

———•—•———

The Lady of the Lake from *Arthur and his Knights* (Mackenzie) *opposite*

'I ask that you get for me Olwen, daughter of Ysbaddaden Chief Giant. And I invoke her in the name of all your warriors.'

Then Culhwch called upon every one of Arthur's warriors by name: Cei and Bedwyr, Cynddylig the Guide and Tathal Frank-deceit, Gwrhyr Fat-kine and Isberyr Cat-claw, Canhastyr Hundred-hands and Llwch Windy-hand, Gobrwy son of Echel Big-hip, and Echel Big-hip himself. He called upon the nineteen sons of Caw and the five sons of Erbin; he called upon Teliesin Chief of Bards and Manawydan son of Llyr, upon Samson Dry-lip, Llawnrodded the Bearded, Hyfeidd One-cloak and Eiddon the Magnanimous.

More than two hundred men were named by Culhwch; on and on he spoke, evoking his boon and calling upon each warrior in turn. He called upon Morfran, son of Tegid – to whom no man dared give a weapon at the battle of Camlan, for he was so exceedingly ugly that all thought he was a devil helping. He called upon Sandde Angel-face – no one gave him a spear at Camlan either, for he was so exceedingly fair that all thought he was an angel helping. He called upon the sons of Erim and upon Glwyddyn the Craftsman, who built Arthur's hall, and upon Gruddlwyn the Dwarf and Gwrhyr Interpreter of Tongues. In the name of all these and many more did Culhwch, son of Cilydd, invoke his boon.

'Ah, chieftain,' said Arthur, ' I have never heard of this maiden of whom you speak, nor of her parents. But I will gladly send messengers to search for her.' So messengers were dispatched and searched for Olwen, but after a whole year they had found nothing.

In the meantime, many received their boons from Arthur and went away happy. 'Everyone has received his boon,' said Culhwch, 'yet I am still lacking mine. I will go away and take the honour of this court with me.'

Lancelot lies sleeping under an apple tree from
Arthur and his Knights (Mackenzie) *opposite*

'You should not try to harm Arthur's reputation, chieftain,' said Cei, 'for the fault is not his. Come with us. Until you say the maiden does not exist, or until we find her, we will not be parted from you.'

Cei had the gift of holding his breath under water for nine days and nine nights, and of going without sleep for the same length of time. It was also said that no physician could heal a wound inflicted by his spear. To accompany Culhwch and Cei, Arthur called upon five warriors who also had special gifts: Bedwyr, who never shrank from any enterprise which Cei undertook and who drew his sword faster than any other knight in battle; Cynddylig the Guide, who was as good a guide in a strange land as he was in his own; Gwrhyr Interpreter of Tongues, who knew every tongue that was spoken; Gwalchmei son of Gwyar, who never came home without having achieved the quest he set out on and who was the best of walkers, the best of riders, and who was Arthur's nephew; and finally, Menw son of Teirgwaedd, who was a master of spells and could make any one of the party invisible should the need arise.

Culhwch and the warriors took their leave of Arthur and rode off on their quest. They travelled until they reached a wide open plain and saw in front of them the greatest fort in the world. All day they journeyed towards this fort and by evening thought they were close to it, but found that they were no nearer than they had been at the beginning of the day.

The second and third days they journeyed on until eventually, with difficulty, they came to that part of the plain where the fort stood. As they approached they saw a great flock of sheep stretching across the plain as far as their eyes could see.

On top of a mound stood the shepherd and at his side a shaggy mastiff that was bigger than a nine-year-old stallion. It was to this fearsome dog's credit that he had never lost a single lamb, let alone a fully grown sheep. The dog would let no one pass, however, and any who attempted it was likely to be torn apart by his massive jaws. Neither would he tolerate any dead trees or bushes on the plain, but burnt them to the ground by the heat of his breath.

'Go and have a word with that man,' said Cei to Gwrhyr Interpreter of Tongues.

Gwrhyr looked at the shepherd's dog. 'Cei,' he said, 'I will not promise to go any nearer than you would go yourself!'

'Do not be afraid,' said Menw, the master of spells, 'I will cast a spell over the dog so that he cannot harm any of us.'

Culhwch and the six warriors then rode to where the shepherd stood on his mound and the huge dog ignored them. 'Things are well with you, shepherd?' asked Gwrhyr Interpreter of Tongues.

'There is none to do me harm except my wife,' the man replied.

'Whose sheep are you are tending? And to whom does that fort belong?'

'What fools of men you must be!' said the shepherd scornfully. 'Everyone in the world knows that this is the fort of Ysbaddaden Chief Giant.'

'And you – what is your name?'

'Custennin son of Mynwyedig,' replied the shepherd. 'Who are you?'

'We are messengers of Arthur, and we have come to seek Olwen.'

'Whew, men! God protect you!' cried the shepherd. 'That is the last thing in the world you should do. No one has ever come to make that request and gone away with his life.'

Hoping to gain more information about Olwen, Culhwch gave the shepherd a gold ring. The man took it home to his wife and invited the travellers to accompany him. When they arrived at the shepherd's gate, his wife rushed out joyously to meet them and would have thrown her arms about their necks in welcome if Cei had not seized a great log from the wood pile and thrust it between her hands. She squeezed it with such force that it was reduced to a withered, twisted twig resembling nothing more than a piece of hemp. 'Woman!' said Cei, 'if you had squeezed me like that I would have had no need for another hug ever. An ill love, that!'

The woman led them into the house, and while they were freshening themselves from their travels, she lifted the lid of a large coffer beside the hearth. Out of it stepped a lad with curly yellow hair.

'Why, what a pity to hide a lad such as this!' said Gwrhyr.

'I hide him because he is all I have left,' said the woman sadly. 'Twenty-three sons of mine have been killed by Ysbaddaden Chief Giant and I have little hope of saving this one.'

'Let him stay with me,' said Cei. 'I swear he shall not be killed unless I am killed too.'

They sat down to eat and the woman asked them on what errand they had travelled so far.

'We have come to seek Olwen,' Gwrhyr replied.

'Then for God's sake go back before you are seen from the fort,' said the woman in dismay.

'We shall not go back until we've seen the lady. Does she ever leave the fort?'

'She comes here every Saturday to wash her hair,' the woman admitted. 'And in the bowl where she has washed it she leaves all her rings. Neither she nor her servants ever collect them.'

'Will she come here if she is sent for?'

'She trusts me, and I swear I shall never betray her, but if you pledge your word that you will do her no harm, I will send for her.'

'We pledge it.'

So Olwen was sent for, and she came. She wore a flowing robe of flame-red silk and her lovely neck was decked with precious stones. Her hair was yellower than the broom flower, her cheeks redder than the reddest foxglove, her breasts whiter than the breast of the white swan. There was none fairer than she and all who saw her loved her.

She entered the house and sat between Culhwch and the high seat at the head of the table. As soon as he saw her, he felt that he knew her.

'Ah maiden, I have always loved you,' he said tenderly. 'Will you come with me?'

'I cannot,' she replied, 'for my father has made me swear an oath that I shall never leave without his permission, for he will live only until I take a husband. But I will give you some advice. Go and ask my father for my hand in marriage, and whatever he demands of you, promise to get it. Then you shall win me. But beware, if you have any doubts, you will be fortunate if you escape with your life.'

'I promise,' said Culhwch eagerly, 'I shall obtain anything your father demands.'

When she returned to the fort, Culhwch and the warriors followed her. They killed nine gatemen at nine gates without one of them crying out, and they killed nine fierce mastiffs without one of them squealing. Then they went into the hall of the fort where they met the giant. 'In the name of God and man, greetings to you Ysbaddaden Chief Giant,' they said with great courtesy.

'And where are you going?' demanded the giant.

'We are going to find your daughter, Olwen, for Culhwch son of Cilydd.'

'Where are those rascally servants and ruffians of mine?' grumbled the giant. The servants appeared with alacrity. 'Raise up my two eyelids with the forked stakes so that I may see my future son-in-law,' Ysbaddaden ordered. This they did. The giant peered at Culhwch and his companions with his one good eye. 'Come back tomorrow,' he said, 'and I will give you my answer.'

As they rose to leave, the giant seized one of three poisoned spears that were near at hand and hurled it after them. But Bedwyr caught it and hurled it back at him, piercing him through the knee.

'You cursed son-in-law!' yelled Ysbaddaden Chief Giant. 'The poisoned iron hurts like the sting of a gadfly! Cursed be the smith who fashioned it!'

That night the travellers lodged in the house of Custennin, the shepherd, and the following day they entered the giant's hall with much pomp. 'Ysbaddaden Chief Giant, give us your daughter. If you refuse to give her, you shall meet your death!'

'She has four great-grandmothers and four great-grandfathers still living,' said the giant. 'I must take counsel with them.'

'Very well,' said Gwrhyr, on behalf of them all. 'Let us now go and eat.'

As they rose to leave, Ysbaddaden seized the second poisoned spear and threw it after them. But Menw caught it and hurled it back at him, so that it pierced the middle of his breast and came out in the small of his back. 'You cursed son-in-law!' screamed the giant. 'The hard iron hurts like the bite of a big-headed leech. Cursed be the forge where it was heated!'

Culhwch and the warriors went to eat, and on the third day they returned to the giant's court and addressed him. 'Ysbaddaden Chief Giant, do not shoot at us again – for if you do, you face injury and death.'

'Where are my servants?' demanded the giant. The servants came running. 'Raise my eyelids with the forked stakes so that I may take a look at my future son-in-law.'

This was done, and then Culhwch's company rose to leave. As they did so the giant took the third poisoned spear and hurled it after them. This time Culhwch caught it and hurled it back, piercing Ysbaddaden through the ball of his eye so that the spear came out through the nape of his neck.

'You cursed son-in-law!' shrieked the giant. 'Now, when I walk into the wind my eyes will water, and I shall have headache and giddiness each new moon. Cursed be the forge where the spear was heated, for the pain where I am pierced is like the bite of a mad dog.'

Culhwch and the warriors went to eat. The following day they returned to the giant's court and again they addressed him. 'Do not shoot at us again, for if you do you will only bring harm upon yourself. Give us your daughter.'

'Who is it,' demanded the giant, 'who has been told to seek my daughter?'

'It is I who seek her, Culhwch son of Cilydd.'

A chair was brought for Culhwch, and when he was seated it was raised up so that he was face to face with the giant. 'When I have got all the things I shall list for you, then you shall have my daughter.'

'Name whatever you will,' said the youth.

'You have seen that great thicket behind my castle?' asked Ysbaddaden. Culhwch replied that he had seen it. 'I must have that cleared and sown in one day, in preparation for the wedding guests.'

Despite the daunting size of the thicket Culhwch did not falter, for he remembered Olwen's words. 'It is easy for me to do that,' he said, 'although you think it is not easy.'

'If you think that is easy, here is something you will not get. I must have Amaethon, the great ploughman, to till and prepare the land. He will never come of his own free will and you cannot compel him.'

'It is easy for me to do that,' said the youth, 'although you think it is not easy.'

The giant continued to list his demands, each following hard upon the other. He required Amaethon's brother, Gofannon the great smith, to set the irons for the plough, and three teams of oxen to be yoked to the plough. He required a measure of buried flax seed, which no man could find, to be grown on the ploughed land to make Olwen's head-dress, and honey from a swarm of virgin bees to be gathered to make bragget (a drink of honey, spices and ale) for the wedding feast. He also asked for a cup of plenty containing the best of all drinks, a plate on which every man would find the meat he desired, a horn of plenty with which to serve the drinks, a cauldron in which to boil the meat and a self-playing harp to entertain the wedding guests.

To each demand Culhwch replied – with a confidence he did not always feel – that it was easy for him to get that, though Ysbaddaden may think it wasn't.

'Even if you get all that, there is yet something you cannot get,' said the giant. 'I must have the tusk from a wild boar with which to shave myself for the wedding. The tusk must be from Ysgithyrwyn Chief Boar and it is no use to me unless it is plucked from his head while he is alive.'

'It is easy for me to get that, though you think it is not easy,' said Culhwch, and his voice was steady.

'I must dress my beard before I can shave,' said the giant, 'and it will never settle unless I use the blood of the Black Witch from the head of the Valley of Grief in the uplands of Hell.'

'It is easy for me to get that, though you think it is not easy,' replied Culhwch, and he did not tremble.

'My hair, too, must be dressed,' said the giant, 'and it is so stiff and tangled that nothing in the world can unravel it, save the comb and shears that are between the ears of Twrch Trwyth, the wildest of all boars.'

Culhwch said it was easy for him to get that too. And so the list continued: fierce dogs with which to track down the boar; Mabon son of Modran as houndsman to hold the dogs; the chief huntsman of Ireland to hunt Twrch Trwyth; Gwyn son of Nudd as huntsman to go with him, and the black horse belonging to Moro Oerfeddawg for Gwyn to ride.

Ysbaddaden went on to name other men, dogs and horses who must be obtained in the quest for Twrch Trywth, and then quickly added various wives, daughters and servants for good measure. Finally, he demanded the sword of Wrnach the Giant, the only weapon with which he could be killed.

'In seeking these things you will never sleep,' he told Culhwch. 'You will not get them, nor will you get my daughter.'

'My lord and kinsman, Arthur, will get them for me,' the youth replied. 'I shall win your daughter and you shall lose your life!'

Culhwch and his companions set out at once and journeyed all that day. At evening light they saw a huge stone fort that must have been one of the greatest forts in the world. They rode up to the gate and Gwrhyr Interpreter of Tongues questioned the man who stood there. 'Is there a porter?'

'There is,' the man replied, 'for I am he.'

'Then open the gate.'

'I will not, for knife has gone into meat and drink into horn and the company is assembled in Wrnach's hall. The gate will not be opened again tonight unless it is for a craftsman that brings his craft.'

'Well, porter, I have a craft,' said Cei, 'I am the best polisher of swords in the world.'

'I will go and tell that to Wrnach the Giant and bring you his answer.'

The porter bore the news to Wrnach who said that he had long been seeking someone to polish his sword. 'Let that man in, since he has a craft.'

So the porter opened the gate to Cei, who went inside all alone. He greeted Wrnach the Giant most courteously. 'Is it true,' said Wrnach, 'that you know how to polish a sword?'

'Indeed I do,' Cei replied. The sword was brought to him. He took a striped whetstone from under his arm and cleaned and polished one side of the blade to perfection. Then he handed the sword to Wrnach the Giant. 'Does that satisfy you?'

'Why, man, I would have it all like this! It is a shame that a man as good as you should be without a companion.'

'I have a companion,' said Cei quickly, 'although he does not practise the same craft. Have the porter admit him, good sir, and I will tell you of his skills. The head of his spear will leave its shaft, draw blood from the wind and then settle upon the shaft again, so swiftly he makes it speed. A wonderful gift has my companion, Bedwyr.'

The gate was opened to admit Bedwyr, and with him came the shepherd Custennin's only son. The rest of the company refused to be parted from these two and killed all who tried to stop them, without the giant knowing.

Cei finished polishing the sword. Wrnach examined the work and expressed satisfaction with it. 'It is your scabbard that has damaged the sword,' said Cei. 'If you give it to me I will remove the wooden side pieces and make new ones for it.'

He took the scabbard in one hand and the sword in the other and approached the giant as if he would place the sword in the scabbard. But suddenly he brought the sword down on Wrnach's neck and sliced off his head at one blow. Then he and his companions destroyed the fort and left, taking with them as many treasures as they could carry.

They travelled for one year to the day, and at the end of that time they came to Arthur's court, carrying the sword of Wrnach with them. Arthur readily agreed to lead them on their various quests, starting with the search for Mabon son of Modron.

'Gwrhyr Interpreter of Tongues, we shall need your skills,' said Arthur, 'for you can speak with the birds and the beasts. Now, let us set out on this quest!'

They went on their way until they came to the Ouzel of Cilgwri. Gwrhyr asked her if she knew anything of Mabon son of Modron, who was stolen away from his mother when only three nights old.

'When I first came here I was very young,' said the ouzel (a small thrush-like bird) 'and there was an anvil here. No work has been done on it, except by my own beak, and today there is barely enough of it left on which to crack a nut open. In all that time I have never heard of the man you seek. Nevertheless, I will do what is right and proper for Arthur's messengers. There is a creature that God made before me and I will take you to him.'

The creature was the Stag of Rhedynfre, and upon reaching him the ouzel explained their quest. 'We have come to you,' she said, 'since we know of no animal older than you.'

'When I first came here,' said the Stag of Rhedynfre, 'there were no trees except for a single oak sapling and it grew into an oak tree with a hundred branches. Then that oak fell and today there is nothing left of it but a red stump. From that day to this I have been here but I have heard nothing of the man you seek. Nevertheless, as you are Arthur's messengers, I will take you to a creature that God made before me.'

The stag took them to the Owl of Cwm Cawlwyd and asked her if she knew anything of Mabon son of Modron, who was taken from his mother when only three nights old.

'If I knew I would tell you,' said the owl. 'When I first came here, this great valley was a wooded glen and a race of men came and laid it waste. A second wood grew up and this is the third. Yet from that day to this I have heard nothing of the man you seek. Nevertheless, as you are Arthur's messengers, I will take you to the oldest creature in the world: the Eagle of Gwernabwy.'

When they came close to the eagle's eyrie the owl left them, and so Gwrhyr Interpreter of Tongues asked the eagle if he knew anything of Mabon son of Modron.

'When I first came here,' said the Eagle of Gwernabwy, 'I had a stone, and from its top I pecked at the stars each evening. Now it is less than a hand's breadth in height, yet from that day to this I have heard nothing of the man you seek. At some distance from here is the Salmon of Llyn Llyw, with whom I have made peace after many years of enmity. Unless he knows something of the man you seek I know none who may. Nevertheless, I will be your guide to the lake where he dwells.'

The eagle led them all the way to Llyn Llyw and addressed the salmon who was swimming there. 'Salmon of Llyn Llyw, I have come to you with Arthur's messengers to ask if you know anything of Mabon son of Modron, who was taken from his mother when only three nights old?'

'What I know, I will tell you,' the salmon replied. 'With every tide I go up the river till I come to the bend of the wall of Caer Loyw and there I have heard such sounds of distress as I have never heard before. You may hear them yourself, for I can carry one of you on each shoulder.'

So Cei and Gwrhyr Interpreter of Tongues rode on the salmon's shoulders until they came to the wall of Caer Loyw. On the other side of the wall a man was imprisoned in a stone fort and wailed piteously at his fate. 'Who is it that laments so in this house of stone?' called Gwrhyr to the prisoner.

'Alas, there is cause enough for him to lament!' came the reply. 'It is I, Mabon son of Modron, who am imprisoned here, and never was a prisoner more cruelly treated.'

'Is there hope that you would be released in return for gold or silver or through battle?'

'If there is any hope for my release at all, it will only be by fighting.'

Cei and Gwrhyr returned to their companions and all of them rode with speed to tell Arthur of their discovery. Arthur summoned his warriors and led them to Caer Loyw where Mabon son of Modron was held prisoner. Cei went again upon one shoulder of the salmon, and this time Bedwyr rode with him on the other shoulder. While Arthur's warriors attacked the fort, Cei broke through the wall and took Mabon on his back, fighting with his enemies as he carried him to safety. So Arthur returned home with Mabon a free man, and Mabon agreed to be houndsman and hold the dogs as the giant had demanded.

Gwyn son of Nudd now had to be persuaded to be huntsman, but he was in conflict with Gwythyr son of Greidawl. Gywn had carried off Gwythyr's maiden by force, whereupon Gwythyr had gathered together an army and come to fight him. Prisoners were taken on both sides and and the conflict still raged, but Arthur devised a means by which the two lords could be reconciled. He decreed that the maiden should live with her father, unmolested by either suitor. Gwyn and Gwythyr should battle for her once a year, on the first day of May, until doomsday. Whoever was the victor on doomsday would win the maiden. So the two rivals were at peace on every day of the year except May Day, and Gwyn son of Nudd agreed to be huntsman as the giant had demanded.

It was Gwythyr son of Greidawl who obtained the flax seeds the giant required, and this he did by chance. He was journeying over a mountain one day when he heard the wailing of hundreds of small voices and saw black smoke coming from an anthill. Springing forward and drawing his sword, Gwythyr struck the burning top from the anthill and so saved the tiny creatures from the fire. 'You have God's blessing and ours,' said the ants, 'and the seeds of flax which no man can find, we will find for you.'

They found the buried flax seeds and brought them to Gwythyr. Only one seed was missing from the full measure that the giant had demanded. A lame ant brought that seed in before nightfall.

Arthur, meanwhile, had successfully obtained many more of those things that the giant required, including the steed of Gweddw, the dogs of Glythfyr and the leash of Cors Hundred-claws. He then sailed to Ireland and seized the cauldron of Diwrnach the Irishman. He brought it back to the shores of Wales filled with the treasures of Ireland.

Then Arthur went after Ysgithyrwyn Chief Boar, leading the hunt with his own dog, Cafall. One of Arthur's warriors rode to the attack, halting Ysgithyrwyn Chief Boar for the first time and bringing him to bay. He then set upon the boar with a hatchet, splitting open his head and removing the tusk. But it was Arthur's dog, Cafall, who finally killed the boar.

When Ysgithyrwyn Chief Boar was slain, Arthur sent Menw, son of Teirgwaedd, to see if the comb and shears were between the ears of Twrch Trwyth. It would be dishonourable to fight the boar if he did not possess the treasures that the giant required.

Twrch Trwyth and his piglets were known to be in Ireland, where they had already laid waste to a third of the country. Menw went to look for them in the likeness of a bird, so that he could fly over Twrch Trwyth's lair and snatch one of the treasures away from him. But he succeeded only in grabbing one of the boar's bristles, whereupon Twrch Trwyth rose up and shook himself vigorously, causing some of his poison to fall upon Menw who carried the scars with him for the rest of his days.

Arthur gathered together all the warriors of Britain and as many as could be mustered from France, Brittany and Normandy. He then picked the best dogs and horses he could find, and when all these were assembled he made his way to Ireland.

The saints of Ireland asked for his protection, which he gave, receiving their blessing in return. The men of Ireland brought him gifts of food and provisions. Then Arthur and his hosts came to the lair of Twrch Trwyth and his seven piglets, and the dogs were let loose from every side.

All that day the Irish fought with Twrch Trwyth, but the boar still managed to lay waste one of the five provinces of Ireland. The following day Arthur's warriors fought with him, but they had no success and many of them were injured. On the third day Arthur himself fought with the boar, and continued to fight with him for nine days and nights, but only managed to kill one of the piglets. Arthur's men were amazed at the mighty strength of Twrch Trwyth, and asked Arthur about him.

'He was a king,' Arthur told them. 'But his wickedness was so great that God transformed him into a pig.'

Arthur then sent Gwrhyr Interpreter of Tongues to have a word with the boar. Gwrhyr, like Menw, went in the form of a bird, and perched above the lair of Twrch Trwyth and his young pigs. 'For the sake of He who made you this shape, if you can speak, I beseech one of you to come and talk with Arthur,' Gwrhyr pleaded.

A piglet called Grugyn Silver-bristle answered. 'By He who made us this shape, we will do nothing for Arthur!' he said. 'God has made us suffer enough by giving us this shape, without you coming to fight us as well.'

'Be warned, Arthur will fight for the comb, the razor and the shears which are between the two ears of Twrch Trwyth,' said Gwrhyr.

'Those treasures will not be taken from him until his life is taken,' Grugyn Silver-bristle replied. 'Tomorrow morning we will set out for Arthur's country, and there we will make all the mischief we can.'

The following morning Twrch Trwyth and his piglets set out by sea towards Wales. Arthur, with his men, horses and dogs, boarded his ship, Prydwen, and very soon caught sight of the boar, who went ashore at Dyfed. Arthur landed further along the coast and then he and his men went in hot pursuit of the boar. But Twrch Trwyth overtook them during the night, killing as many men and cattle as he could before Arthur arrived to protect them.

Arthur then sent his men to the hunt, his champions and best dogs to the fore and Bedwyr with the dog, Cafall, among them. Twrch Trwyth set out from Glyn Nyfer and came to Cwm Cerwyn, where he stood at bay and killed four of Arthur's champions. Held at bay again, he wounded four more of them before being wounded himself.

The following morning at dawn some of Arthur's men caught up with the boar. He killed the three servants of Glewlwyd Mighty-grasp, Arthur's chief porter, and among them was Penpingion who went upon his head to spare his feet. After that he killed many more, including Gwlyddyn the Craftsman, Arthur's chief builder. He went on to kill Cynlas son of Cynan, Gwilenhin king of France, Glyn Ystun and then the men and dogs lost him.

Arthur summoned Gwyn son of Nudd and asked him if he knew anything of the boar's whereabouts, but Gwyn said he did not. All the huntsmen then went as far as Dyffryn Llychwr in search of the pigs, and there Grugyn Silver-bristle and his brother, Llwydawg the Hewer, took them by surprise, dashing in amongst them with such force that only one man was left alive.

Arthur and his men reached the two piglets and released all the dogs upon them. Such a clamour then ensued that Twrch Trwyth came in defence of Grugyn Silver-bristle and his brother, bringing his other piglets with him. Immediately he was set upon by men and dogs, and although he fought with all his might, his piglets were killed, one by one, until only Grugyn Silver-bristle and Llwydawg the Hewer were left alive to escape with him.

Arthur caught up with them at Llwch Ewin, where Twrch Trwyth killed Echel Big-hip and many a man and dog besides. Grugyn Silver-bristle separated from them there, but was pursued by the huntsmen and killed at Garth Grugyn. His brother, Llwydawg, went on to Ystrad Yw and there he killed the king of Llydaw and two of Arthur's uncles before being killed himself.

Arthur summoned the men of Cornwall and Devon to meet him at the mouth of the River Severn. 'Twrch Trwyth has slain many of my men,' he said. 'But while I live he shall not attack Cornwall. I shall pursue him no further, but will fight with him to the death.'

A number of horsemen and dogs were sent to beat the boar back towards the Severn, and by sheer force they drove him into the river. Mabon son of Modron went in after him on Gwyn Dun-mane, the steed of Gweddw, and Menw went also. Arthur and the champions of Britain fell upon the boar, and Osla Big-knife closed in on him – with the help of Arthur's servant, Cacamwri, and several warriors. First, they took hold of the boar's feet and held him in the river until the water was flooding over him. Then Mabon son of Modron spurred his horse and took the razor from between the boar's ears. Cyledyr the Wild, on another horse, plunged into the Severn and took the shears. But before anyone could seize the comb, Twrch Trwyth found land with his feet, scrambled out of the river and neither dog nor horse could keep pace with him as he fled into Cornwall.

Arthur and his warriors pursued the boar until they caught up with him, and after suffering further loss and injury among themselves they finally won the comb from him. Twrch Trwyth was then forced out of Cornwall and into the Irish Sea and nobody knows what became of him.

When Arthur had bathed and refreshed himself, he asked if there were any of the giant's demands which remained unfilled. 'Yes,' said one of his warriors, 'we do not have the blood of the Black Witch, daughter of the White Witch, from the head of the Valley of Grief in the uplands of Hell.'

So they set out northwards until they came to the hag's cave, and on the advice of Gwyn son of Nudd and Gwythyr son of Greidawl, Cacamwri and his brother, Hygwydd, were sent in to fight with the witch. As Arthur's servant and his brother entered the cave the hag grabbed at them, catching Hygwydd by the hair and throwing him to the ground beneath her. Cacamwri then seized the witch by her hair and dragged her away from Hygwydd, but she turned upon them both ferociously, disarming them and driving them squealing from her cave.

Arthur was angry to see his two servants almost killed. He would have gone in to battle with the witch himself, had not Gwyn and Gwythyr told him that it would not be seemly for him to scuffle with a hag. He therefore sent two more of his men into the cave, but these two fared even worse than the first, and all four had to be loaded on Arthur's mare, Llamrei, before they could leave.

Then Arthur stood at the entrance to the cave and took aim at the hag with his knife, Carnwennan, striking her across the middle and cutting her clean in two. Her blood was collected and thus the quests set by Ysbaddaden Chief Giant were finally completed.

Culhwch set out at once for the giant's court, taking with him all the marvels Ysbaddaden had demanded. With him went Goreu, the only living son of the shepherd Custennin, and others who wished ill to the giant.

'Have you had your shave?' Culhwch asked him.

'I have,' Ysbaddaden replied.

'And is your daughter mine now?'

'She is,' he said. 'But do not thank me for that; thank Arthur who has won her for you. And it is now time to end my life.'

Goreu, son of Custennin, caught the giant by the hair and dragged him to the mound on the plain, where he cut off his head and set it up on a stake for all to see. Then he took possession of the giant's fort and all his lands.

That night Culhwch slept with Olwen and she remained his wife for as long as he lived. Arthur's armies dispersed to their own lands. And that is the story of Culhwch son of Cilydd, who won for his bride the beautiful daughter of Ysbaddaden Chief Giant.

Gareth and Lynette

From Alfred Lord Tennyson's *Idylls of the King*

THE 'KNIGHT OF THE KITCHEN'

THE THREE KNIGHTS
OF THE STREAM

THE KNIGHT WHO CALLED
HIMSELF DEATH

LYNETTE: …because thou strikest as a knight;
Being but knave, I hate thee all the more.
GARETH: Fair damsel, you should worship me the
more; That, being but knave, I throw thine
enemies.

(In Act Four Margawse is known as 'Bellicent', in accordance
with the original source material for this section.)

areth was the youngest and tallest son of King Lot and Queen Bellicent. He had grown from boy to man and yet, at his mother's request, he remained at home. The spring months had been full of showers and the river near his parents' hall was swollen and flowing fast. He watched as a slender pine was uprooted and swept away by the flood.

'How it went down!' he said to himself, 'just as an evil knight would have gone down before my lance. If, indeed, I had a lance of my own to use,' and he sighed deeply. 'I am grown now and should be free, yet I remain a spoiled and pampered prisoner in my mother's house, for she still treats me as a child. So my good mother is a bad mother to me! Surely it would be better to have a worse mother? But no, she is mine and I would not change her. Yet I shall go on wearying her by begging for my freedom. O, to fly the nest and soar up, eagle-like, to the great glorious sun – and then swoop down on all things base and destroy them. A knight at Arthur's court, to do his bidding to make the world a better place. Why, when my two brothers Gawain and Mordred came here last summer, Gawain asked me to tilt (joust) with him – and he a proven knight of Arthur's! As no one worthier was at hand, Mordred was our judge, and I so shook Gawain in his saddle that he declared me to be half-way the victor. Mordred, of course, was tight-lipped and silent as usual, but he is always sullen.'

Then Gareth went home to his mother and knelt beside her chair. 'Sweet mother,' he said, 'though you count me still a child, tell me this – do you love the child?'

She laughed at him affectionately. 'You are a goose to question it,' she said.

'Then, mother, if you love the goose – will you hear his story?'

'Yes, my beloved one, of course I will. Is it of the goose and golden eggs?'

'No, no, mother, this story is about an eagle perched upon a palm tree almost above eye-reach. A poor youth forever hovered round the palm and saw the treasure sparkling from on high and thought, "If I could climb up and lay my hand upon that treasure, I should be richer than the richest kings." But whenever he stretched out a hand to climb, one who had loved him from his childhood stopped him, saying, "Do not climb, I beg you, by my love, lest you break your neck." And so the boy neither climbed nor broke his neck, but broke his heart instead by pining for that treasure.'

'Why, whoever loved him truly from his childhood should have taken all the risk,' the mother replied, 'and climbed up and handed down the golden treasure to him.'

'Golden? Did I say gold? The thing I spoke of was of greater worth than gold: it was that true steel from which they forged the sword Excalibur. And lightning played about it in the storm and all the little birds were flurried by it, and there were cries and crashings in the nest that would drive you from your senses. O, let me go, sweet mother!'

Then Bellicent became sorry for herself. 'Have you no pity for my loneliness?' she asked. 'Look at your father lying by the hearth like a log. Ever since he fought against the king and then Arthur gave him back his territory, he has aged beyond belief. Now he lies there, a corpse, yet unburiable. He neither sees, nor hears, nor speaks. And I have no one else, for your two brothers have gone to Arthur's hall – though I swear I loved neither of them as I love you. Stay here, for you are an innocent who has never known so much as a finger-ache, and to think of you in jousts and wars with wrenched or broken limbs terrifies me to the very heart. Stay and follow the deer by our tall firs and fast-flowing burns. The chase is sweet and I will find you a beautiful bride when the time is right. Stay, my best son! You are barely more than a boy yet.'

'Follow the deer!' cried Gareth, becoming angry. 'No, mother, I must follow Arthur, the king.'

'There are many who do not believe him to be king,' Bellicent replied. 'Or, at least, will not deem him to be fully proven king. In my own heart I know him to be royal, for I was with him frequently in my youth and I doubted him no more than he doubted himself. Yet will you leave your easy life here and risk everything for one who is not even proven king? Stay, at least until the cloud that surrounds his birth has lifted a little. Stay, sweet son.'

'Not for an hour longer!' said Gareth passionately. 'Though I will walk through fire to gain your permission to go. Not proven king, you say? Why, he swept away the dust of ruined Rome, crushed the idol worshippers and made the people free. Who else should be king if not the one who gave us our freedom?'

The queen realised her son was unwavering in his determination. 'You will walk through fire?' she said craftily. 'Go then, if you must. But before you ask the king to make you a knight, I demand one proof of your obedience and love to me, your mother.'

'Whatever you demand, I shall go,' Gareth replied. 'So hurry! Ask what you will.'

But Bellicent took her time in answering, looking at him closely as she spoke. 'You shall not go to Arthur's hall as a prince, but disguised as a servant to do menial chores and serve meat and drink among the scullions and the kitchen-hands. Nor shall you tell anyone your name until you have worked in that manner for one year and a day.' She awaited his reaction, convinced that he was too proud to accept such a condition and would remain at home with her.

Gareth was silent awhile before replying. Then he said, 'Though physically enslaved, I should still be free in spirit. And I shall see the jousts. I am your son, mother, and therefore I yield freely to your will. I shall go, disguised as you require, and serve with scullions and kitchen-hands. And I shall tell no one my name – not even the king.'

He did not leave immediately, for his mother looked at him with such sad and troubled eyes that his resolution almost broke. But he was awakened early by the wind blowing through the darkness, and arose at once and awoke two of his own faithful servants. The three then dressed themselves as farm labourers and left together while his mother still slept.

They set off south towards Camelot with the melody of early morning birdsong all around them as they went. The rising sun restored the damp slopes to a living green, among which many flowers opened their petals to the warm sun, for it was now past Easter.

When they reached the plain before Camelot, they saw the royal city rising through the silver-misty morning; sometimes the spires and turrets pierced the mist, but at other times they could see only the great shining gate that opened on the field below. 'Let us go no further, lord,' said one of Gareth's companions, overcome by fear. 'This is a city of enchanters, built by fairy kings.'

'It is said at home in the north that this king is not a king at all,' added the second man, 'but a changeling from fairyland, who drove the heathens away by sorcery and Merlin's magic.'

'My lord, there can be no such city anywhere,' the first man insisted. 'It is just a vision!'

Gareth laughed at them. 'I have enough magic in my own blood and youth and hopes to throw old Merlin into the Arabian sea!' he said, pushing his reluctant companions towards the gate.

There was no other gate like it in all the world. A statue of the Lady of the Lake surmounted the arch above it, the sacred fish swimming in water that flowed over her dress and dripped from her hands. From one of her hands a sword hung down. On either side of her were depicted scenes of Arthur's wars, but in such a weird and timeless manner that men were dizzied by just looking at them. High on top of all else were the figures of the three queens who would help Arthur in his time of need, and about everything were entwined strangely carved creatures and unworldly figures.

Gareth's companions stared at these figures for so long that it seemed as if the dragons' tails and weird carvings began to move and seethe. 'Lord!' they called to Gareth, 'the gateway is alive!'

Gareth, too, had looked for so long that even to his eyes they seemed to move. Suddenly, a blast of music pealed forth from the city and the three men started back from the gate in alarm. Then an old man with a long white beard came through the gateway and approached them. 'Who are you, my sons?' he asked.

'We are tillers of the soil,' Gareth replied. 'We have left our labours to come and see the glories of our king. But your city seemed to move so strangely in the mist that my men here doubt whether the king is really the king at all, but rather one who has come from fairyland. And they wonder if there is really any city at all, or if it is just a vision. That music we heard just now has scared them both, so will you tell them the truth?'

The old man did not answer Gareth plainly, but teased him with riddles. 'Son,' he said, 'I have seen a ship sail in the heavens, keel uppermost and mast downwards, and solid turrets topsy-turvy in the air. This is the truth, and if you do not like it you may accept what you have told me as the truth, for as you say, a fairy king and queen have built the city. They came from a sacred mountain bringing with them the knowledge of mysterious arts from the east, and each carrying a harp, and they built the city to the music of their harps. You are right; it is enchanted, for nothing within is what it seems, except the king. Yet some will say the king is a shadow and the city real. But heed the king well, for when you pass beneath this archway you will be within the spell of his enchantment. The king will bind you by such vows as it is dishonourable for any man to break, yet which no man can keep. And if you are afraid to swear to such vows do not enter this gateway, but stay outside like a beast in the field. If you heard music, then it is likely they are building still, since the city was built to music and being built to music was never built at all, and therefore built for ever.'

Gareth was angered by the old man's obscure words. 'Old master,' he said, 'you should honour your beard, which being so very long and white seems to promise truth. Why do you mock a stranger who asks a civil question?'

'Do you not know the Riddling of the Bards?' asked the ancient one. 'Confusion and illusion and relation? Elusion and occasion and evasion? I do not mock you, but you mock me and all who see you, for you are not what you seem to be. But I know you for who you are; and now you go to mock the king, who cannot even tolerate the suspicion of a lie.'

Merlin – for that is who the old man was – turned away from them and passed out of sight along the plain. Gareth watched him go, thoughtfully, before turning to address his men. 'Our one white lie haunts us on the threshold of our adventure,' he said. 'Let us blame love for it, not my mother. But we shall make amends.'

Then he laughed with good cheer and led his two companions into Camelot. It was a city of shadowy places and rich, stately carvings of stone, showing the deeds of ancient kings. Everything was touched by the magic of Merlin's hand, and the pinnacles and spires seemed to rise to the sky. Knights passed to and from the great hall with a clashing of metal armour – a sound that was good to Gareth's ear. Fair maidens peeped shyly out of bowers and everywhere people stepped respectfully, as if in the presence of a gracious king.

As he entered the long-vaulted hall, Gareth heard Arthur's voice and then saw the king himself, throned in splendour and passing judgement upon the fates of those who came before him. The youth trembled, wondering if the king would condemn him for his one small lie. He looked for his brothers, Sir Gawain and Sir Mordred, but could see neither of them, although many other tall knights stood about Arthur's throne.

A widow came before the king begging for a boon (gift) because King Uther, Arthur's father, had taken her husband's field. 'First Uther offered us gold,' she said, 'but the field was useful to us and we refused, so then he took it from us by force and left us neither field nor gold.'

'And would you have the field?' Arthur asked her. 'Or would you sooner have the gold?'

The woman wept, remembering her husband. 'The field, my good lord,' she said, 'for it was important to my husband.'

'Then have your field again,' Arthur replied. 'And three times as much gold as Uther offered for it. This is no boon, but justice, for cursed be the man who would not right his father's wrongs.'

Many others came before him also, including a king who would have harmed Arthur had he not been prevented, whereupon Arthur instructed Sir Kay, the seneschal (steward), to attend to this king's wants and offer him food and wine. Others came crying noisily to the king, begging redress or a boon, and for each of these humble petitioners a knight would ride away, bent upon some quest.

Last of all came Gareth, leaning heavily on the shoulders of his two men. 'A boon, Sir King,' he said, and his voice was filled with shame. 'For you see how weak I am with hunger. Allow me, I beg you, to serve meat and drink among your kitchen-hands for one year and a day – and do not ask my name. After that, I will fight.'

'So fine a youth is worth a finer boon!' said Arthur. 'But if you will ask for nothing better, then Kay, the master of meat and drink, shall be your master also.'

The king rose and left the hall and Kay, a mean-spirited man, turned to some of the other knights. 'Look now!' he cried. 'This fellow must have escaped from some abbey, where I swear he did not get enough beef or brewis (broth). Well, I care little for that – if he works well for me, I'll cram him full of food until he is as sleek as any hog.'

One of Arthur's finest knights, Sir Lancelot, was standing close by. 'Sir Seneschal,' he said to Kay, 'you know all manner of hounds and you know horses, but it seems you do not know a man. Look at this boy's brow, his fine wide nostrils and fair hands; a lad of mystery, perhaps, but whether from a sheep-pen or a palace he has a noble nature. Treat him with goodwill, or one day you may be ashamed of your judgement of him.'

'What do you mean by mystery?' asked Kay. 'Do you think he may poison the king's supper? No, he spoke too much like a fool. Mystery, ha! If the lad were noble he would have asked for a horse and armour. Fine and fair indeed! Sir Fine-face? Sir Fair-hands? Look to your own fineness, Lancelot, lest it prove your undoing – and leave my man to me.'

So Gareth, true to his mother's wish, suffered the greasy work allotted to a humble servant of the kitchen. He ate with the young lads by the door and slept at night with grimy kitchen-hands. Whenever Sir Lancelot saw the youth he always spoke to him pleasantly but Kay, the seneschal, disliked him and hustled and harried him and set him the most arduous and unpleasant tasks.

Gareth found some solace in kitchen gossip when he heard the servants praise the love between Lancelot and the king. They told how the king had saved Lancelot's life twice in battle and Lancelot had saved the king's once – for Lancelot was the greatest knight in tournament, but Arthur was the mightiest on the battle-field. But if the talk of the kitchen-hands became base, then Gareth would whistle as loudly as he could. At first his fellow servants laughed at him for this, but before long they began to respect him.

For a month Gareth lived and worked in the kitchen. But in the weeks that followed his departure, Queen Bellicent repented the servitude she had imposed upon her son and sent word, by a squire of Lot's, to say that she released him from his vow. Overjoyed, Gareth sought a private audience with the king and told him everything. 'I have shaken even your strong Gawain in a tilt,' he said eagerly. 'I can joust. Make me your knight – in secret. Let my name be hidden and give me the first quest.'

The king looked at him closely and Gareth, blushing, fell to his knees and kissed the royal hand. "Your good mother, the queen, let me know that you were here,' said Arthur. 'And she expressed the wish that I should yield to your request. Make you my knight? My knights are sworn to vows of boldness, of courage, gentleness and, in loving, of utter faithfulness. And they are sworn to uttermost obedience to the king.'

'My lord, courage and boldness I can promise you,' said Gareth, springing lightly from his knees. 'As for love, although I do not love yet, I shall do so, God willing. And for uttermost obedience only ask the one to whom you gave me: the seneschal. No easy master of meat and drinks is he! So have I not earned my cake in the baking of it?'

Arthur smiled, warming to this lusty, eager young man. 'Make you a knight in secret?' he said. 'Yes, but there is one who must know – our most noble brother and truest knight.'

'Lancelot? O let Lancelot know, my lord. Let Lancelot know! For the rest, leave me unnamed until I have made my name. My deeds will speak; it is but for a day.'

Laying a kindly hand on Gareth's arm, the king agreed to yield to his request and made him a knight. Then he summoned Lancelot into his presence. 'I have given the boy the first quest,' he told his favourite knight. 'He is not proven, and when he calls for it, mount your horse and follow him. Cover the emblems on your shield so that you will not be recognised, and follow him as far as you can to see that he is neither taken nor killed.'

Later that morning a lady of high birth entered the hall, accompanied by her page. She was very fair, her brow as white as May blossom and her cheek as pink as apple blossom and her small nose tip-tilted like the petal of a flower.

'O King!' she cried to Arthur. 'Why do you sit here? If I were king I would not rest until the most remote castle in the land was freed from bloodshed.'

'Comfort yourself,' Arthur replied. 'I do not rest and neither do my knights; they keep the vows they swore to make the wildest moorland of our kingdom as safe as the inside of this hall. What is your name, lady? And what is your need?'

'My name is Lynette, my lord, and I need a knight to fight for my sister, Lyonors, a lady of high birth and great estate – and one more beautiful than I. She lives in Castle Perilous, and a river surrounds her castle in three loops, with three bridges crossing it. Three knights, who are brothers, defend the bridges while a fourth brother, the mightiest knight of all, holds her prisoner in her own castle until she agrees to marry him. She will only wed a man she loves, and yet this knight remains until you send your chief man, Sir Lancelot, to do battle with him. He expects to defeat Lancelot. Therefore I have come for Lancelot's help.'

Arthur, remembering that he had promised the first quest to Gareth, questioned the lady further. 'Lady, who are these four knights? What sort of men are they?'

'A very foolish sort. They ride abroad, recognising neither law nor king, and do as they please – courteous one moment and bestial the next. Three of them – those who defend the bridges – call themselves after the day: Morning Star, Noonday Sun and Evening Star. The fourth, who always rides in black and is a huge, savage man-beast, calls himself the Night or, more frequently, Death. He wears a helmet mounted with a skull and has a skeleton figured on his arms. All four are fools, my lord, but fools of mighty strength. And so I have come for Lancelot.'

Whereupon Sir Gareth – as he was now called – rose to his feet, taller than all the rest, and called out, 'A boon, Sir King! Grant me this quest as a boon!' Then hearing Kay, nearby, groan like a wounded bull, he said, 'Yes, I am your kitchen-hand, and mighty through your meat and drink. I can topple more than a hundred such mighty fools. Remember your promise, my lord!'

For a moment Arthur frowned at this outburst. 'Rough and impetuous!' he said. Then his brow cleared. 'But pardonable nevertheless, and worthy of a knight. Therefore, go!'

All who heard this were amazed, but the lady was furious.
'For shame, my lord!' she cried. 'I asked for your chief knight and
you have given me only a kitchen-hand!'

Before anyone could prevent her, she turned and fled from the
hall and the king's presence. She did not pause until she had
passed through the weird gate and mounted her horse. There
was, however, another exit from the great hall and out of this
Gareth strode puposefully, to be confronted with a sight that
filled his heart with joy, for there stood the king's gift to him. It
was the finest warhorse he had ever seen, prepared and ready to
mount. Beside this horse were his two faithful servants, bearing
his full armour, a shield and a spear.

Gareth donned the armour, took the shield and mounted his
horse. People then crowded about him and the servants came
running from the kitchen, delighted to see one who had worked
among them mounted and in arms. 'God bless the king and all
his company!' they cried lustily, throwing their caps into the air.

So Gareth rode joyfully between the throngs of cheering people
and out through the massive gate. There was one, however, who
did not cheer. Sir Kay stood sullenly watching the young man
ride away in glory.

'Bound upon a quest with horse and arms!' he muttered
scornfully. 'The king must be out of his mind! Come thralls
(humble servants), back to your work, for if you let the kitchen
fire burn low you will fuel my fires of anger.'

The servants departed in haste. When they had gone, the
seneschal continued to mutter resentfully. 'Go forth! Worthy to
be a knight! Some old head wound, unheeded in his youth, must
have so shaken the king's wits that they wander in his prime and
he is crazed. How that villain lifted his voice to bawl out
shamelessly that he was a kitchen-hand. Tut! This is your doing,
Lancelot. The knave was meek enough with me till you took
notice of him and puffed him up like a peacock. Well, I will ride
after the loud-mouthed knave and see whether he knows me for
his master yet. He came out of the smoke, and if my lance does

its work, he shall go into the mire and from thence – if the king recovers from his madness – back into the smoke again.'

'Kay,' said Sir Lancelot sternly. 'Will you go against the king? This lad was always obedient to you, humbly serving the king through you. Wait! Take counsel, for the boy is fine and agreeable and understands both lance and sword.'

'Do not tell me that!' snapped Kay. 'You are too willing to spoil humble knaves with foolish praise.' He then mounted his horse and rode through the now silent crowd and out beyond the gate.

There was one other who muttered disconsolately to herself. By the tournament field the lady still lingered. 'Why did the king scorn me?' she fumed. 'For even if Sir Lancelot was not available, he might have given me one of his other proven knights. But, oh, shame upon him, to offer me his kitchen-hand!'

At that moment Sir Gareth drew level with her, shining in his new armour. 'Lady, the quest is mine,' he said. 'Lead and I follow.'

She held her dainty nose between thumb and finger as if smelling something foul. 'Keep your distance!' she said. 'For you smell of kitchen grease. And look who follows you.'

Kay rode up and reined his horse in beside them. 'Do you not know me?' he taunted the young knight. 'I am Kay, your master, and we need you at the kitchen fires.'

'Master no more!' Gareth replied. 'And I know you only too well, as the unkindest knight in Arthur's court!'

'I challenge you, then!' cried Kay, and straightaway rode hard at Gareth. But the younger man was too quick for him and countered his attack with his own spear, so that the two came together with a mighty clash. Kay was thrown from his horse, wounded in the shoulder.

'Lead, and I follow,' cried Gareth to the damsel. She spurred her mount and rode away from him as fast as she could, pausing only when her horse was exhausted by the violent exertion.

'What are you doing in my company, scullion?' she demanded, as Gareth overtook her and reined in his horse. 'Do you think I respect you more or like you better because, by some cowardly trick, you have overthrown your master? Dish-washer and pot-stirrer! You fool – to me you still smell only of the kitchen.'

'Lady,' Gareth answered gently, 'say what you will, but whatever you say I shall not leave you until I finish this fair quest or die in the attempt.'

'Will you finish it?' Lynette asked scornfully. 'Sweet lord, how like a noble knight he talks! By listening to his betters the rogue has caught the manner of it. But I tell you this, knave, you will meet one so fearful that, for all the kitchen broth you have supped, you will not dare to look him in the face!'

'Then I shall be truly put to the test,' said Gareth with a smile. This maddened the maid still further, and she spurred her horse and flashed away again. Gareth followed her down the long avenue of trees until at length she paused, bemused.

'Sir Kitchen-knave,' she said. 'I have missed the only path where Arthur's men are set to protect travellers through this wood. The wood is as full of thieves as leaves, and if we are both killed at least I shall be rid of you. But yet, Sir Scullion, can you use that spit of yours?' she waved an impudent hand towards his spear. 'Fight if you can – I have missed the only path.'

So the two rode on until dusk when, after mounting one long slope, they saw a gloomy, shaded hollow among pine trees, with a lake in the deepest part of it, from which arose the sound of shouting. Suddenly, a servant broke through the dark trees crying wildly, 'They have tied up my master to cast him in the lake!'

Gareth vanquishes the Red Knight, watched by Lynette
from *Arthur and his Knights* (Mackenzie) *opposite*

'I am bound to fight for those who are wronged,' Gareth said to the lady, 'but even stronger is my bond to stay with you.'

'Lead and I follow,' Lynette replied contemptuously.

'Follow then, I lead!' cried Gareth, and he plunged down among the dark pines.

In the shadows by the lake, thigh-deep in rushes and reeds, six tall men were hauling a seventh man into the water, with a stone about his neck to drown him. Gareth set upon the villians with his lance and felled three of them while the other three fled through the pines. The young knight loosed the stone from the seventh man's neck and tumbled it into the oily waters of the lake, then he released the man's bonds and set him on his feet.

'Had you not come,' said the man, an honourable baron and a friend of Arthur's, 'those vile rogues would have wreaked vengeance on me. They have good cause to hate me, for whenever I catch a thief I drown him here with a stone about his neck. Many of their own kind lie beneath this water rotting, but at night they let go the stones and rise, dancing eerily on the lake, flickering in the grim light. It is good that you have saved my life, for I have some worth as the cleanser of these woods. I will gladly reward you handsomely. Tell me then, what reward will you have?'

'None!' Gareth replied sharply. 'I have done the deed for the sake of doing it and in uttermost obedience to the king. But will you offer shelter to this lady?'

'Why, I do believe you are from Arthur's Round Table,' said the baron, whereupon Lynette gave a small laugh.

Lancelot and Guinevere together for the last time from
The Idylls of the King (Eleanor Fortescue Brickdale) *opposite*

'That is truth of a sort,' she said, 'being Arthur's kitchen-hand.'
She turned to Gareth. 'Do not think I accept you any more,
scullion, for running with your spear upon a group of wicked
thieves. Indeed, a harvester with his threshing-flail could have
scattered them as well. And you still smell of the kitchen. But if
this lord will give us shelter, that is well.'

They rode with the baron to his mansion, a league (about three
miles) beyond the wood. There had been a feast that day and
there was plenty of food left which was very welcome to the two
late guests. A roasted peacock in his pride (with tail feathers left
on) was placed in front of Lynette, and the baron sat Gareth
beside her. But she rose at once.

'You have shown me much discourtesy, Lord Baron, by setting
this knave at my side,' she said. 'Hear me, for this morning I
stood in Arthur's hall and begged him to give me Lancelot to
fight the evil brothers of Day and Night. The latter, who also
calls himself Death, is unconquerable by any save the one for
whom I asked, Sir Lancelot. Then this shameless kitchen-hand
calls out, "The quest is mine, I am your kitchen-hand and
mighty through your meat and drink." And Arthur, suddenly
gone mad, replies, "Go forth," and gives the quest to him.
Him! This villian here – one who is more fitted to stick swine
than to ride abroad redressing ladies' wrongs, or to sit beside a
noble gentlewoman.'

The baron, embarrassed and amazed, looked from Lynette to
Gareth and back again. Then he left the lady to the peacock and
seating Gareth at another table, sat down beside him.

'My friend,' he said, 'whether you are a kitchen-hand or not, or
whether it is the lady's imagination, and whether she is mad or
the king is mad, or both or neither, or you yourself are mad –
I do not ask. But you strike a mighty blow, you are strong and
courageous and here, if you wish, there are mighty men to joust
with. Will you not turn back with your lady and ask the king to
let Lancelot go in your place? You will, I trust, forgive my
presumption – I speak only to try and benefit one who has saved
my life.'

'I thank you and ask your full pardon,' Gareth replied graciously,
'but I must continue my quest to overcome Day and Night.'

So the following morning the baron accompanied them for a
short way on their journey, then wished them God speed
and left them.

'Lead, and I follow,' Gareth said to the damsel as before.

'I shall not run from you this time,' she told him haughtily, 'for
the most unlikely creatures will share an island, for a brief hour,
in time of flood, and I feel some pity for you now. Will you not
turn back, fool? For near here is one who will overthrow and kill
you. Then I shall return to Arthur's court and make him
ashamed for having given me a defender from the ashes
of the hearth.'

'Have your say, and I will do my deed,' Gareth replied
courteously.

They reached the shore of one of the long loops of the river that
encircled Castle Perilous; the bank was steep and heavily
wooded, and the full stream was spanned by a bridge forming a
single arc. On the other side of the stream was a bright pavilion
of silk, decked with gold and with a red banner fluttering on top
of a purple dome. Before this pavilion paced the lawless knight
who called himself Morning Star. 'Lady!' he called to Lynette.
'Is this the champion you have brought from Arthur's hall?
The one for whom we let you pass?'

'No, no, Sir Morning Star!' Lynette called back. 'The king has
shown utter contempt for your foolishness and sent you his
kitchen-hand. Beware that he does not fall upon you suddenly or
kill you unarmed, for he is not knight but knave.'

'Daughters of the Dawn and servants of the Morning Star,
approach and arm me,' called the knight on the other side of the
stream. Three lovely maidens, bare-footed and bare-headed,
came from within the silk pavilion, clad him in blue armour
and then handed him a shield of blue. Gareth stared at the

impressive figure of Morning Star as he stood waiting for his horse to be brought to him.

'Why do you stare so?' demanded Lynette. 'Are you frightened? There is still time to flee before he mounts his horse. No one would be surprised; after all, you are not a knight but a knave.' 'Lady,' said Gareth, 'whether knave or knight, I would fight twenty such as he sooner than hear you speak of me so. Kind words would be best for your defender, yet truly I believe cruel words are better, for they send such strength of anger through me that I know I shall defeat that knight.'

The blue knight was now mounted. 'A kitchen-knave, sent in scorn of me!' he cried from across the bridge. 'I do not fight such as he, but return scorn with scorn. It would be a shame to do more than take his horse, disarm him and send him back to the king. Come, then, knave – leave the maiden, for it is not seemly for a knave to ride with such a lady.'

'You lie! My ancestors are nobler than your own!' Gareth replied angrily.

The two knights then rode full tilt at each other to meet in the centre of the bridge with an impact that unseated them both. For a moment they lay stunned, then quickly rose to their feet and drew their swords. So fiercely did Gareth lash at his opponent that he drove him backwards down the bridge. 'Well struck, kitchen-knave!' cried Lynette.

The Morning Star then lashed at Gareth's shield, breaking it into two pieces, but Gareth countered the attack with one swift sword stroke, laying his enemy grovelling on the ground. 'Do not take my life – I yield!' cried the stricken knight.

'I will grant your life willingly if this lady asks it of me,' said Gareth.

Lynette reddened. 'Insolent scullion!' she cried. 'I, ask anything of you? I shall not be bound to you for any favour.'

'Then he dies,' said Gareth, and unlaced the other knight's helmet as if to kill him.

'Wait, scullion!' she shrieked. 'Do not be so audacious as to kill one nobler than yourself.'

'Lady, your request is a pleasure to me,' said Gareth. 'Knight, your life is saved at her command. Arise and go speedily to Arthur's court. Say his kitchen-hand has sent you. See that you ask his pardon for breaking his laws; I shall plead for you myself when I return. And I will have your shield.' He took the blue shield and bade farewell to the defeated knight. 'Now, lady – lead, and I follow.'

She sped ahead of him and when he caught up with her, she said 'I thought, knave, when I watched your sword-play upon the bridge just now, that the smell of your kitchen was a little fainter. But the wind has changed and I smell it twenty times more strongly. Therefore I say begone with you, take my advice and flee. Hard by here is a knight who guards a ford – the second brother – and he will prove more than a match for you. Do not fear that fleeing will shame you, for you are not a knight but a knave.'

'Knight or knave,' said Gareth, 'the knave that does you service as a knight is every bit as good as a knight for freeing your sister, Lyonors.'

'Yes, Sir Knave!' she mocked. 'But because you strike as boldly as a knight, I despise you all the more for being a knave.'

'Fair maid,' he replied, 'you should admire me more, that being but a knave I overthrow your enemies.'

'Yes, yes,' she said impatiently, 'but you will meet your match.'

They came to the second river-loop and there, beyond a raging shallow, was a huge knight mounted on a great chestnut horse. His armour was so highly polished that it dazzled the eye, and his shield flashed with a fierce brightness, as if from the rays of the sun. 'What are you doing, brother, here in my regions?' roared the knight who called himself the Noonday Sun.

'No, no,' Lynette answered, her voice shrilling above the raging waters. 'He is a kitchen-hand from Arthur's hall, and he has overthrown your brother and taken his arms.'

'Ugh!' cried the Noonday Sun. He lifted his vizor to reveal a ruddy face of rounded foolishness, and then spurred his horse across the foaming ford to be met by Gareth in midstream. There was no room here for lance or tournament skills, the two knights struck four strokes with their swords – and so mighty were the strokes that Gareth feared he may be defeated. Then, as the Noonday Sun lifted a ponderous arm to strike the fifth stroke, his horse's hoof slipped in the stream and the Sun was washed away.

Gareth lay his sword across the ford and drew the drenched knight to safety. But the Noonday Sun fought no more; his bones had been so battered on the rocks that he yielded at once to his adversary, and Gareth sent him to the king. 'I will plead for you myself when I return,' the young knight told him, and then he turned to Lynette. 'Lead, and I follow,' he said.'

This time she did not race away from him but led quietly. 'Hasn't the wind changed again?' Gareth asked her.

'No, not at all, nor are you the victor here. His horse stumbled on a ridge of slate under the water. I saw what happened myself.' Then she began to sing *O Sun!*' explaining that she was not singing of the strong fool whom Gareth had overthrown.

'O Sun, that wakenest all to bliss or pain,
O moon, that layest all to sleep again,
Shine sweetly; twice my love hath smiled on me.'

She turned to Gareth, 'What do you know of love songs or love? But if by God's grace you had been nobly born, I might have said you have a pleasant manner.' She sang on.

'O dewy flowers that open to the sun – what do you know of flowers, except to garnish meats with? O birds, that warble to the morning sky – what do you know of birds, except those that are for the spit, for larding and basting? Well, you may have cooked your last unless you turn now and fly, for there stands the third of the brothers.'

Beyond a bridge with three arches, seemingly naked and glowing rose-red in the late sunlight, stood the knight who called himself the Evening Star. 'Why does that madman stand there naked while it is still daylight?' said Gareth in amazement.

'He is not naked,' Lynette replied, 'he is wrapped in skins that fit him like his own, and they are so hardened that they will turn the blade of your sword if you try to pierce them.'

The third knight saw the shield that Gareth had taken from the Morning Star. 'O brother star,' he called from across the bridge, 'why do you shine in my region? Your own is further up the river. But have you killed this lady's champion?'

'He's no star of yours,' Lynette called back, 'but one shot from Arthur's heaven to bring disaster to you. Both your younger brothers have fallen to this youth, and so will you, Sir Star. Are you not old?'

'Old and hard, lady,' replied the third knight. 'Old with the might of twenty boys.'

'Old and over-bold in bragging!' said Gareth. 'But that same strength which threw the Morning Star can overthrow the Evening.'

The other knight blew a loud and dismal note upon a horn and shouted, 'Approach and arm me!' whereupon an old woman staggered out of a stained and storm-beaten pavilion, carrying a suit of worn and rusted armour. She armed the knight and put a helmet with a crest of drying evergreen upon his head, then handed him a shield bearing the crest of the Evening Star – half tarnished and half polished.

The two knights hurled themselves at each other on the bridge and Gareth overthrew the other, then dismounted, drew his sword and overthrew him again. The older knight was not readily defeated, however, but started up like fire and battled fiercely. Each time Gareth brought him to his knees he vaulted up again. The young knight panted with effort and his heart laboured. He seemed to strike at his enemy without direction.

All the while, Lynette shouted encouragement. 'Well done, knave-knight, well struck, oh good knight-knave! Do not shame me – strike, for you are worthy of the Round Table. Strike – his arms are old, he trusts his hardened skin. Strike, strike – the wind will never change again!'

Hearing this, Gareth struck more strongly with his blade, hewing great pieces of armour off his opponent. But he lashed in vain against the hardened skin beneath the armour and could not completely bring the third knight down. The two fought on, from side to side and up and down the bridge, until at last Gareth's blade clashed mightily against the other's sword and broke it to the hilt. 'I have you now!' he cried jubilantly. But the older man sprang forth and, in a manner most unknightly, writhed his wiry arms about the youth till, despite his armour, Gareth felt almost strangled. Straining to his uttermost, he cast his attacker from him and hurled him headlong over the bridge, and the Evening Star was swept away by the river to sink or swim.

'Lead, and I follow!' Gareth cried.

'I no longer lead,' said the damsel quietly, 'but ask you to ride here at my side. You are the kingliest of all kitchen-knaves – I would add knight, had I not heard you call yourself a knave. Sir, I am ashamed to have been so rude to you. I am a noble lady and I thought the king had scorned both myself and my family; now I ask your pardon and friendship, for you have always answered me courteously and you are as brave and gentle as any of Arthur's best.'

'Lady, you are not all to blame,' said Gareth generously, 'except for mistrusting the good king and thinking he would scorn you or give you a defender unfit to cope with your quest. You spoke your mind and my deeds were my answer. By heaven, a man is no knight and certainly not worthy to fight for any gentle lady if he allows her wayward words to turn his heart to bitterness. Ashamed, you say? There is no need for shame. Your foulest words fought for me, and now that you speak fair words to me I swear there is not a knight – not even the great Sir Lancelot himself – who has the strength to quell me.'

It was now evening. Lynette turned to Gareth and smiled at him. 'There is a cavern close by,' she said, 'where the Lady Lyonors has had bread, meat and red wine put out for her coming champion. It awaits you now, Sir Knave, my knight.'

They passed through a deep valley in which figures of knights and horses had been carved in the slabs of rock. 'A hermit lived here once,' Lynette explained, 'and it was his holy hand that fashioned in the rock the war of time against the soul of man. Follow the faces of these figures and we find the cave. But, look! Who rides up behind us?'

It was Sir Lancelot, who had helped the injured Kay back to Arthur's hall, and then been further delayed because Lynette had missed the correct path through the woods. Now, having swum the river-loops, he had caught up with the young knight and his lady. But, seeing the blue star on Gareth's shield he mistook him for the defeated Morning Star and cried angrily, 'Stay, wicked knight! I avenge you for my friend.'

Gareth turned to do battle with his challenger, and because Lancelot had obeyed the king and covered the emblems on his own shield, he did not recognise him. They closed, Gareth felt one touch of that spear, handled with a skill that was the wonder of the world, and fell easily to the ground, laughing as he clutched the grass between his fingers.

His laughter irritated Lynette. 'Shamed and overthrown,' she cried, 'and tumbled back into being a kitchen-knave. Why do you laugh? Is it because your boast was all in vain?'

'No, fair lady,' Gareth replied. 'It is because I, the son of old King Lot and good Queen Bellicent, victor of the two bridges and the ford, and knight of Arthur, now lie here thrown by an unhappy chance or some sorcery – and by whom, I do not know.'

'Gareth!' said Lancelot in dismay. 'Why, prince, it is you – thrown by the unhappy chance of Lancelot, who came to help, not to harm you. But how happy I am to find you as whole as on the day that Arthur knighted you.'

'You, Lancelot – your hand threw me! Why, if I had gone down before a lesser spear I should be ashamed, but oh, Lancelot, you!'

Lynette did not share the mutual pleasure of the two knights. 'Lancelot,' she said petulantly, 'why did you not come when you were called? And why do you come now when you are not called? I admired my knave who, even when rebuked, answered as courteously as any knight. But if he is indeed a knight the marvel dies, and leaves me fooled and tricked. I think I have been scorned after all, for where else should I expect to find the truth but in Arthur's hall and in Arthur's presence? Knight, knave, prince and fool – now I hate you more than ever.'

'O lady, you are not wise to call him shamed because he is overthrown,' said Lancelot. 'I have been thrown myself, not once but many times. Blessings upon you, Sir Gareth, for you are such a knight as the king would wish for, and although you and your good horse are tired, I felt your strength through that weary lance of yours. You have done well, for the stream is free and you have dealt justice for the king, answered graciously when insulted and made merry when overthrown. Welcome, prince and Knight of our Round Table.' Then, turning to Lynette, he told her Gareth's full story.

'Oh well,' she said, 'I suppose even worse than being fooled by others is to fool oneself,' and she shrugged off her petulance. 'Sir Lancelot, there is a cave close by with food and drink and hay for the horses. It is surrounded by honeysuckle, and if we seek we shall find it.'

They sought and found the cave by the sweet-scented flowers, and Gareth ate and drank and then fell into a deep, exhausted sleep. 'Sleep soundly,' said Lynette, 'and waken refreshed, for you have good cause to sleep. Do I not seem as tender to him as any mother? But a mother who has reprimanded him angrily all day long and then blesses him in sleep. Ah, how sweet the honeysuckle smells in the still night, as if the world were filled with utter peace and love. O Lancelot, Lancelot, I am truly pleased to find my knave is a noble knight. But if the black enemy who calls himself Death does not let me pass, I have sworn to bring you to do battle with him. Now he will see you first, and who can doubt that you will be the victor? So my knight-knave will miss the chance to accomplish this final deed.'

'The one you name may know my shield,' said Lancelot. 'I will let Gareth change his shield for mine and take my horse, which is fresher and needs no spurring, loving the battle as much as his rider does.'

'You are courteous in this, Lord Lancelot, as in all things,' said Lynette gratefully.

When he awoke, Gareth clutched Lancelot's shield fiercely. 'How well I shall care for this,' he said, 'and respect the emblem upon it. From my hold on this shield, Lancelot, will come virtue and fire – and I shall not shame even its shadow. Now, let us go.'

They travelled silently across the quiet night fields and, glancing up, Gareth saw a shooting star. 'Look!' he cried, 'the enemy falls!' Then an owl hooted among the trees. 'Hark!' cried Gareth, 'the victor's voice rings out!'

Suddenly, Lynette became fearful and clung to Lancelot's shield. 'Give it back to him,' she pleaded. 'He is the one who must fight. I curse the tongue that insulted you all through yesterday and has now begged Lancelot to lend you shield and horse. You have done wonders but you cannot perform miracles. There is glory enough in having overthrown the three brothers; now I fear you will be maimed and mangled, for I swear you cannot overthrow the fourth.'

'And why not, lady? Tell me all you know of him. You cannot scare me; the roughest face or voice, huge size or brute savagery will not turn me from this quest.'

'I never saw his face,' Lynette replied, 'for he never rides by day, but I've watched him passing like a phantom in the night. I never heard his voice, for he has a page who comes and goes and always speaks for him. And this same page tells of his dreadful deeds – how, when he is angry, he will slay men, women and children; some even say that he has eaten the flesh of babes. He is a monster! I went for Lancelot first and the quest is his. Give him back his shield.'

'If he fights me for it,' said Gareth, laughing. 'For then he would most likely win it as the better man, but that is the only way.'

Lancelot, however, urged the young knight to put into practice all the strategies of chivalry, managing horse, lance, sword and shield, and so succeeding with skill and finesse where force might fail.

'I know only one rule,' Gareth admitted, 'and that is to dash against my enemy and win. But I have watched your victories in the jousts and observed your ways.'

'Heaven help you!' sighed Lynette.

They rode on for a while, under clouds that dimmed the stars. Then Lynette halted her mount, lifted an arm and whispered, 'There!'

All three were silent, seeing, in the gloom, a huge black pavilion like a mountain peak pitched on a flat field before the Castle Perilous. A black banner fluttered languidly on top and a long black horn hung down beside it.

Gareth seized the horn, and before the other two could prevent him, raised it to his lips and blew into it with all his breath. The walls of the castle echoed to the sound and lights appeared in the windows. Gareth again blew upon the horn. Soon they heard muffled voices and feet tramping up and down, and saw shadows flitting past. High above them, encircled by her serving-maids, the Lady Lyonors stood at a window, beautiful among the lights, waving graciously to the young knight below.

After Gareth had blown upon the horn for a third time there was a long hush, and then slowly the black drapes of the pavilion opened and a monstrous figure appeared, seated high on a night-black horse. Crowned with a grinning skull and decked with white breast bone and the bare ribs of death, the figure advanced some ten paces and then paused, but did not speak.

'Fool!' said Gareth angrily. 'They say you have the strength of ten men, so why not trust the limbs that God has given you, instead of tricking yourself out with ghastly images from the grave?'

The hideous rider remained silent, and a lady fainted. The Lady Lyonors wrung her fair, white hands and wept, fearing she was doomed to be the bride of Night and Death. Gareth's scalp prickled beneath his helmet – even Sir Lancelot felt ice strike through his warm blood – and all who saw the fearsome figure were aghast.

Lancelot's charger neighed fiercely, with Gareth in the saddle and ready for battle. Death bounded forward on his dark war-horse, and those who did not hide their eyes in terror, saw that he was cast to the ground and then slowly rose. But with one stroke Gareth split the hideous skull in two so that half fell to the right and half to the left, and both halves lay grotesquely on the ground. Then with a mightier stroke he cracked open the helmet as thoroughly as the skull – to reveal the fresh, bright face of a young lad!

'Do not kill me!' begged the boy, 'for my brothers made me do it to bring a horror to the castle and keep the world from Lady Lyonors. They never dreamt that they would be defeated at the streams.'

Gareth was gracious to this boy, who was only a little younger than himself. 'My fair child,' he said. 'What madness made you challenge the chief knight of Arthur's hall?'

'Sir, they told me to do it. They hate the king and they hate Lancelot, the king's friend. They hoped to kill him somewhere on the stream – they never dreamt the bridges could be passed.'

So the terrible night ended happily. Lady Lyonors threw open her doors, and with dance, revelry and song, everyone made merry over Death, who had proved, after all their foolish fears and horrors, to be no more than a fresh and harmless boy.

Laughter ruled and Gareth won the quest, and as for who won the young knight's heart . . .

'. . . he that told the tale in older times
Says that Gareth wedded Lyonors,
But he, that told it later, says Lynette.'

ACT FIVE

The Death of Arthur

From Sir Thomas Malory's *Morte D'Arthur*,
'The Book of Morgan le Fay', 'The Book of Sir Lancelot and the King'
and 'The Book of the Morte d'Arthur'.

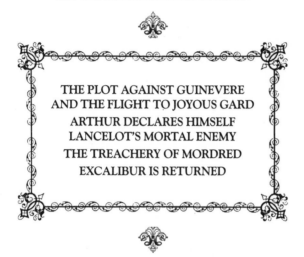

THE PLOT AGAINST GUINEVERE
AND THE FLIGHT TO JOYOUS GARD

ARTHUR DECLARES HIMSELF
LANCELOT'S MORTAL ENEMY

THE TREACHERY OF MORDRED

EXCALIBUR IS RETURNED

SIR LANCELOT: Alas! I have no heart to fight against my lord, King Arthur.

SIR PALOMIDES: My Lord, though you spare them all this day, they will never give you thanks; and if they may get you at any vantage, ye are but dead.

SIR LANCELOT AND THE KING, XIII

Lancelot and Guinevere

ir Agravain and his brother, Sir Mordred – who was King Arthur's son by his half-sister – were among the least popular of the Knights of the Round Table and renowned for bringing ill-fortune to others. It was during the month of May, a time of year that should be joyous, that these two knights brought sorrow and bitterness to King Arthur's court.

They both bore a secret hatred for Guinevere, Arthur's queen, and an even stronger hatred for Sir Lancelot, who was the king's favourite knight. Night and day they watched Lancelot, and then one day, when they were in Arthur's chamber with their brothers, Gawain, Gaheris and Gareth, and various other knights, they spoke out openly.

'It is a wonder,' said Agravain, 'that we are not ashamed to see how Sir Lancelot behaves, for he lies with the queen by day and night, and we all know it is so. I say it shames every one of us that we allow so noble a king as Arthur to be humiliated in this way.'

'Brother,' said Sir Gawain sternly, 'Do not make such accusations. I do not wish to hear them and I will have no part in your scheming.'

Sir Gaheris and Sir Gareth also refused to be drawn into any plot against Sir Lancelot. 'We will not associate ourselves with your actions,' they told Agravain firmly.

'Then I shall!' said Mordred.

'I can well believe it!' Gawain replied. 'For you will agree to any mischief. But I wish that you would both leave all this alone and not interfere, for I know what will come of it.'

'Come of it what may,' said Agravain, 'I shall disclose it to the king.'

'I would not advise it,' replied Gawain, 'for if it came to war between Sir Lancelot and ourselves, mark my words, brother, there are many who would side with Sir Lancelot. You should also remember how many times Sir Lancelot has come to the rescue of the king and queen; indeed, the best among us would long since have been dead were it not for Lancelot. I will never speak against him, for he rescued me once from King Carados of the Dolorous Tower, killing him and saving my life. Also, my brothers Agravain and Mordred, he likewise rescued you and three score other knights from Sir Tarquin. I think such noble deeds and kindness should be remembered.'

'Remember them if you like,' said Agravain sullenly, 'but I shall conceal it no longer.'

At that moment King Arthur entered the chamber. 'Now brothers,' said Gawain urgently, 'cease your strife!'

'That we shall not,' replied Agravain and Mordred in one voice.

'Will you not?' said Gawain. 'Then may God be your guide, for I will not carry your tales nor have anything to do with your plotting.'

'Nor I,' said Gaheris.

'And neither will I,' said Gareth, 'for I shall never say anything to harm that noble man who made me a knight.'

'Alas!' said Sir Gawain, 'now is this realm wholly destroyed and put to shame, and the noble fellowship of the Round Table will be dispersed.'

Gawain, Gaheris and Gareth departed from the chamber and King Arthur asked the remaining knights what had been the cause of their disagreement.

'My lord, I shall tell you,' said Agravain, 'for I can keep it from you no longer. My brother Mordred and I have just revealed to our brothers, Gawain, Gaheris and Gareth, that Sir Lancelot has been sleeping with your queen for a long time. As your sister's sons we can allow it no longer, for we all know that you should be in command of Sir Lancelot. You are the king who made him a knight, and we shall prove that he is a traitor to you.'

'If you speak the truth, then he is indeed a traitor,' Arthur agreed. 'But I would be reluctant to believe such a thing without proof. Sir Lancelot is a bold knight and you all know that he is the best among us. Unless he is caught in the act he will fight with whoever spreads such a rumour, and I know of no knight who can match him. Therefore, if what you say is true, he will have to be caught in the act.'

The king was loath to hear any scandal spoken of Sir Lancelot and his queen, for Lancelot had done so much for Guinevere and himself and Arthur loved him better than any other knight. Yet there was some suspicion in his mind that Agravain's words could be true. Merlin had warned him that this would happen. But Merlin, his friend and counsellor, was no longer with him.

The magician's end had come about exactly as he himself had prophesied. He had fallen for the charms of Nimue, one of the ladies of the lake, and followed her everywhere, uncharacteristically foolish in his lovesickness. She had encouraged him at first, eager to learn his magic arts. And Merlin, in his dotage, had revealed to her all his secrets.

'I shall not endure much longer,' he had told King Arthur, 'for despite all my magic powers I shall soon be imprisoned in the earth.' He went on to warn the king of misadventures that would befall him. 'Keep careful watch upon your sword, Excalibur, and its scabbard,' he said, 'for they will be stolen from you by a woman whom you trust above all others.'

Merlin and Nimue had travelled together over land and sea, and he had shown her many wonders. But by the time they returned to England and went to Cornwall she had grown weary of his passion, and was also a little afraid of him. He showed her a rock where there was an enchanted cave beneath a stone. Cunningly she persuaded him to go under the stone so that she could see the wonders of the cave. Merlin, as ever, did her bidding and she used his own magic to imprison him in the cave. There she left him, incarcerated for all time!

Not only did Arthur deeply regret losing his magician, he also had reason to respect his words. Excalibur had been stolen from him, just as Merlin had prophesied – by none other than Morgan le Fay, the youngest daughter of Igraine, and Arthur's half-sister. Arthur had indeed trusted Morgan implicitly, possibly even more than he trusted his own fair queen, Guinevere.

Morgan le Fay was married to King Urience, but she was passionately involved with Sir Accolon, a knight of Arthur's court. She plotted to kill her husband and make Accolon king. More than any other man in the world she hated her half-brother, Arthur, for the power and respect he held in the realm. If Arthur was killed, Accolon could be king of all England, and she would be his queen.

Morgan le Fay's magical skills were considerable, for she had successfully studied necromancy. Therefore she obtained Arthur's sword, Excalibur, by enchantment, and gave it to her lover. A fight had been arranged between King Arthur and Sir Accolon, without either knight being aware of the other's identity. Morgan sent one of her maidens to Arthur with a sword that looked like Excalibur and its scabbard. He, unsuspecting, accepted the counterfeit weapon and went into battle with Sir Accolon.

Armed with the wondrous Excalibur, Accolon cut and hacked Arthur almost to the point of death, breaking the king's brittle counterfeit sword and leaving him weaponless. Had it not been for the intervention of Nimue – that same maiden of the lake who imprisoned Merlin – Arthur would certainly have died. But for love of King Arthur, the lady used the powers she had learned from his magician, enabling him to retrieve Excalibur, and its scabbard, and win the day.

The fact remained, however, that Merlin had been right about the treachery of Morgan le Fay, so it was possible that he was also right about Lancelot and Guinevere.

'My lord,' said Sir Agravain, breaking in upon the king's reflections, 'if you will announce that you are going hunting tomorrow, I will wager that Sir Lancelot will not ride with you. As darkness approaches, send word to the queen that you will be out all night. During the night, we shall take Lancelot with the queen – and bring him to you, dead or alive.'

'Very well, I agree,' said the king, 'and I advise you to take bold and loyal companions with you.'

'Sir,' said Sir Agravain, 'my brother Mordred and I will take with us twelve knights of the Round Table.'

'Be careful, for I warn you that Lancelot is very strong.'

'We will put our plan into action,' said Agravain.

So the following morning the king rode out hunting and sent word to the queen that he would be out all night. Sir Agravain and Sir Mordred assembled twelve knights, and they all hid themselves in a chamber in the castle of Carlisle.

When night fell, Sir Lancelot told his nephew, Sir Bors, that he was going to speak with the queen.

'Sir,' said Sir Bors, 'take my advice and do not go to the queen tonight.'

'Why?' asked Lancelot, surprised.

'Sir Agravain waits each day to bring shame on you and on us all, and my heart warns me that you should not go to the queen tonight. Sir, I believe the king has only stayed away so that a watch may be put upon you and the queen. Some treason is afoot.'

'Never fear,' said Lancelot, 'for I shall stay briefly with the queen, I shall not linger.'

'That you should go at all worries me,' said Sir Bors. 'I fear it will harm us all.'

'My dear nephew,' said Lancelot, 'I wonder why you should say this, since the queen has sent for me. Should I be such a coward as to refuse to see her?'

'God speed you then,' said Sir Bors, 'and send you back safe and sound.'

Sir Lancelot departed, wearing no armour but only his mantle. When he reached the queen's chamber, she opened her door and he went swiftly inside. While they were together in the chamber, Sir Agravain, Sir Mordred and the twelve knights of the Round Table arrived outside the door, fully armed and prepared for battle. 'You traitor, Sir Lancelot! Now you are taken!' they cried loudly, so that all the court could hear.

Inside the chamber Guinevere paled. 'Alas!' she said, 'now we are both brought to ruin!'

'Madam,' said Lancelot, 'is there any armour in here which I can wear? If there is, give it to me and by the grace of God I shall silence those knights and overpower them.'

'Truly,' said the queen, 'I have no armour; neither helmet, shield, sword nor spear. I am afraid that our long love has come to a shameful end, for I can hear that there are many noble knights outside and I am sure they are well armed. You can do nothing against them, Lancelot. You are likely to be killed – and then I shall be burnt alive!'

'Never was I in such a situation,' said Lancelot. 'That I should be shamefully killed for the lack of my armour!'

'Traitor knight, come out of the queen's chamber!' cried
Sir Agravain and Sir Mordred from outside. 'You know full well
that you are surrounded and cannot escape.'

'I shall not be shamed by such scandal,' said Lancelot angrily.
'A quick death will be better than the pain of enduring these
insults.' He took the queen in his arms and kissed her.

'My most noble Christian queen, I beg you – as you have always
been my special lady and I your truest and most humble knight,
who has never failed you since the day King Arthur knighted me
– I beg that you will pray for my soul if I am killed. I am sure that
my nephew, Sir Bors, the rest of my family and Sir Lavaine and
Sir Urry will not fail to rescue you from the fire. Therefore, my
own dear lady, take courage again, and whatever becomes of me,
go with Sir Bors and Sir Urry. They will render you every service
they can and you shall live like a queen on my lands.'

'No, Lancelot, no,' said Guinevere. 'I swear I shall not live long
without you. If you are killed, I shall take my own death as
meekly as any martyr.'

'Well, madam, since the day has come when our love must end I
shall sell my own life as dearly as I can. I am more distressed for
you than for myself, but I would give anything to have armour in
which to fight so that men may speak of my deeds if I am killed.'

'Truly,' said the queen, 'if God were willing, I would rather that
they kill me and allow you to escape.'

'That shall never be,' cried Lancelot, 'God defend me from
such shame!'

By this time, the knights outside had fetched a massive bench
from the hall and were attempting to batter down the chamber
door with it. Lancelot wrapped his mantle firmly about his arm.
'Fair lords,' he called to them, 'cease your insults and turmoil and
I shall open this door. Then you may do with me as you like.'

'Come on then and do it!' Agravain replied. 'You will gain nothing by fighting against all of us. Let us into the chamber and we will spare your life until you come before King Arthur.'

Sir Lancelot unbarred the door and, with his left hand, held it open a little so that only one man at a time could enter. A large knight, called Sir Colgrevance of Gore, strode forward and struck a mighty blow at Lancelot with his sword, but Lancelot deflected the blow with his right arm – which was protected by his mantle – and, seizing the sword, struck Sir Colgrevance so fiercely upon his helmet that he fell down dead in the chamber doorway. Using his great strength, Lancelot drew the fallen knight into the chamber and there, with the help of Guinevere and her ladies, he was quickly arrayed in Colgrevance's armour.

Meanwhile, Agravain and Mordred were shouting at him from outside. 'Traitor knight, come out of the queen's chamber!'

'Sirs, stop your shouting,' said Lancelot. 'I swear you shall not imprison me tonight, so take my advice, leave the chamber door and let no more be heard of your insults and your slander. I promise you, by my knighthood, that if you go now and go quietly I shall appear before you all, and before the king, tomorrow morning. Then let it be seen which of you shall accuse me of treason. I shall answer you, as a knight should, that I came here to the queen with no evil intention, and I shall prove it to you in combat.'

'Shame upon you, false traitor!' cried Agravain. 'No matter what you do, we shall kill you if we wish, for we have the authority of the king to save you or slay you.'

'If there is no grace with you, then defend yourselves!' replied Sir Lancelot. He threw open the chamber door and, with knightly courage and mighty strength, strode in among them. At the first stroke he slew Sir Agravain and then twelve of his fellows. Within a short while he had killed each one, for none of the twelve could withstand a blow from Sir Lancelot. Only Mordred escaped with his life. He was wounded and fled from his adversary as fast as his legs would carry him.

Then Lancelot turned again to Guinevere. 'Madam,' he said, 'our true love is now at an end, and from this day forth King Arthur will always be my enemy. But if you choose to stay with me, I shall save you from all danger.'

'Sir, that would not be wise,' Guinevere replied sadly. 'It seems you have already done so much harm that it would be better if you go no further. But if tomorrow morning you see they are going to put me to death, I trust you to rescue me as you think best.'

'I will indeed,' said Sir Lancelot. 'Have no doubt that so long as I have breath in my body I shall rescue you.' He kissed her, and each gave the other a ring. Then he left the queen in her chamber and went home to his lodging. He was met by Sir Bors, clad in full armour and declaring that he had never been so glad to see Lancelot return home.

'Jesus have mercy!' said Lancelot. 'Why are you armed? What does this mean?'

'Sir,' replied Sir Bors, 'your family and your friends were so perturbed when you left us that some of us leapt out of our beds naked, and some caught their swords in their hands while they were still dreaming. We believed there was a great battle on hand and that we were entrapped by some treason, so we made ourselves ready to give you whatever help you might need.'

'My dear nephew,' said Lancelot, 'tonight I was surrounded by such hostility as I have never encountered before in my life. But, thanks be to God, I escaped.'

He told Sir Bors and the other knights what had happened. 'Therefore, my friends, I pray you will be of good heart and help me in whatever need may present itself, for now I fear that war is coming to us all.'

'Sir,' said Sir Bors, 'whatever God sends us is welcome. We have enjoyed much wealth with you and much praise; we will now take the woe as willingly as we have taken the wealth.' All the good knights who were present agreed and assured Sir Lancelot of their support.

'Thank you,' said Lancelot gratefully. 'Your words are a great comfort to me. But I would ask you, dear nephew, to find out as quickly as possible which of those near to the king will remain loyal to me and which will not, for I must know who are my friends and who are my enemies.'

'I will do so immediately,' said Sir Bors, 'and by full light I will be able to tell you who will hold with you and who against.'

True to his word, Sir Bors called upon all those knights who would follow Sir Lancelot loyally. He assembled twenty-two such knights from Arthur's court, armed and on horseback and ready to do Sir Lancelot's bidding, and these knights were joined by a further eighty loyal followers from Cornwall and Wales.

'My lords,' said Sir Lancelot, addressing them all. 'You know that ever since I came to this court I have been a loyal friend to my lord Arthur and my lady Guinevere. Last night, my lady the queen sent for me to speak with her, and this has been put about as a treason. There is no blame with the queen, but I was with her by design and would have been killed if God had not protected me.'

He went on to tell them how he had been beset in the queen's chamber by his assailants and how he had managed to escape from them. 'So, my good lords, because I have slain Sir Agravain – who is Sir Gawain's brother – and also twelve of his followers, there remains nothing for me and my kin but war. These knights were sent by King Arthur to betray me, therefore in his anger and malice the king will condemn the queen to the fire. I cannot allow her to be burnt for my sake. If I may be heard and accepted as her champion, I will fight for her to prove that she is a true lady to her lord, the king. But I fear that the king in his fury will not accept me as her champion.'

'My lord, Sir Lancelot,' said Sir Bors, 'it is my advice that you take the rough with the smooth and thank God for it. In view of what has come about, I advise you to look after yourself, for if you guard yourself well there are no knights in the world who can harm you. And, my lord, if my lady Guinevere is to be burnt because of you, then I say you should rescue her, for if you do not, your name will be spoken of in shame by everyone. The fact remains that you were caught with her, and whether you did right or wrong it is now your place to stay loyal to her and ensure that she is not put to death – if she dies, the shame will be yours for ever.'

'Jesus defend me from shame!' cried Sir Lancelot. 'And guard my lady and save her from dishonour and death. She will never be killed through my failure to take up the challenge. So, my lords, what will you do?'

'We will do as you do,' they replied in one voice.

'King Arthur will heed his evil counsellors and tomorrow morning, in his anger, he will put my lady the queen into the fire and burn her,' said Lancelot. 'So, my friends, give me your advice.'

One knight spoke for all of them. 'Sir, you must rescue the queen as a good knight should. If she is burnt, it will be for your sake, and if you are caught it is likely that you will suffer a similar death – or worse. You have rescued the queen many times for other men's quarrels, and therefore it is only honourable that you should rescue her from this quarrel, which is for your sake.'

'My lords, you must know that I would be loath for my lady the queen to die such a shameful death. In order to rescue her, however, I must do a great deal of damage; it is possible that I shall have to kill some of my best friends and I should regret that deeply. But if I do succeed in saving the queen, where shall I keep her?'

'That is the least of your problems,' said Sir Bors. 'You may take the queen to your own castle, Joyous Gard, and keep her there until the king's anger has abated. You may be able to return her to the king with great honour later, and I warrant you shall have his thanks for it, no matter who else remains hostile.'

They all agreed that, for better or worse, if the queen was brought to the fire, they would rescue her. So, by Sir Lancelot's advice, they took cover in a wood as near as possible to Carlisle, and there they waited to see what the king would do.

Mordred, having escaped from Lancelot and run to his horse – sorely wounded and weak from loss of blood – then rode to King Arthur and told him how all were dead except himself.

'Merciful heaven, how can this be?' said the king. 'Did you catch him in the queen's chamber?'

'Yes, God help me,' Mordred replied. 'We found him there unarmed, and then he killed Sir Colgrevance and put on his armour.' And he told the king exactly what had happened.

'Jesus have mercy!' said Arthur, 'Lancelot is a remarkably skilful knight and I am deeply sorry that he should turn against me. Alas! I am sure that the fellowship of the Round Table is broken for ever, for many noble knights will remain loyal to Lancelot.' Then he added, with genuine sorrow, 'Now my honour demands that my queen must be put to death.'

His anger allowed no mercy and the queen was condemned to the fire. In those days, death was the lawful punishment for treason by a person of any rank, and the slaying of Agravain and the twelve knights was evidence against Guinevere.

'My lord Arthur,' said Gawain, who had come before the king with his brother knights, 'I advise you not to be over-hasty and to postpone your judgement of the queen. Although Sir Lancelot was found in the queen's chamber, it may be that he was there for no evil purpose. You know, my lord, that my lady, the queen, is beholden to Sir Lancelot more than to any other knight, for often he has saved her life and done battle for her when all the court refused to help her. So, it is likely that she sent for him to reward him for his gallant deeds to her in the past. And perhaps the queen sent for him in secret only to avoid slander; how often we do things for the best and they turn out to be for the worst. I am sure that your queen is both good and true to you. As for Sir Lancelot, I am certain that he will challenge any knight living who charges him with villainy or treason and that, likewise, he will protect the honour of the queen.'

'I can well believe it!' said King Arthur, 'But the queen shall be punished according to the law. If I capture Lancelot, you can be sure that he will suffer an equally shameful death.'

'May God grant,' said Gawain, 'that I never see it or know of it!'

'Why should you say that?' asked the king. 'Indeed, you have no cause to love him! This very night he killed your brother, Sir Agravain, and he almost killed your other brother, Sir Mordred. And remember, Sir Gawain, that he killed two sons of yours – Sir Florence and Sir Lovell.'

'My lord,' said Gawain, 'I am aware of all this and I grieve for their deaths. But I gave them warning, and told my brother and my sons how it would end. They would not heed my advice and I will take no revengeful action for their deaths, for I told them it was useless to strike against Sir Lancelot. I am sorry for the death of my brother and my two sons, but they brought it upon themselves.'

'I pray you,' said Arthur, 'make yourself ready in your best armour, with your brothers Sir Gaheris and Sir Gareth, to bring my queen to the fire.'

'No, my noble king,' said Gawain, 'that I will not do. I swear that I shall never be present when so noble a lady as Queen Guinevere suffers such a shameful end. My heart will not allow me to see her die, and it shall never be said that I agreed to your plan to burn her.'

'Then,' said the king, 'allow your brothers Sir Gaheris and Sir Gareth to be there.'

'My lord, you know they will not wish to be there,' replied Gawain, 'but they are both young and unable to refuse you.'

'Sir,' said Gaheris to Arthur, 'you may command us to be there, but you must understand that it is sorely against our will.'

Gareth added his agreement. 'We shall be there only by your order, which gives us no choice but to obey. But we will be there in peace and bear no armour.'

'Then in the name of God make ready,' said the king, 'for she shall soon meet her judgement.'

'Alas,' said Gawain, 'that I should live to see this terrible day!' He turned aside and wept without restraint.

The queen was led forth from Carlisle and stripped down to her smock. Then the holy priest came to give her the last rites and there was much weeping among the lords and ladies. Lancelot had sent one of his men to discover at what time the queen would be taken to the stake, and when this man saw her given the last rites, he immediately gave Lancelot warning. At once Sir Lancelot and his band of knights galloped to the place where Guinevere was to die and any who resisted them were killed, for none could withstand the strength of Sir Lancelot.

Among those who bore arms and fought against them were many noble knights, and all of them were slain. In the chaos that ensued, Sir Lancelot charged here and there and, by pure misfortune, chanced to slay Gaheris and Gareth, for both were unarmed and unprepared for battle. Lancelot did not see them and it was not until later that they were found among the dead in the field.

When Sir Lancelot had slain or put to flight all who opposed him, he rode straight to Queen Guinevere, threw a cloak about her and lifted her up behind him on his horse.

So Lancelot rode with the queen to Joyous Gard, and there in his castle he kept her as a good knight should. A number of great lords and noble knights came to him there. When they heard that King Arthur and Sir Lancelot had quarrelled, some of the knights were joyful – but most were saddened by their disagreement.

Arthur and Lancelot at War

hen King Arthur was told how the queen had been rescued from the fire and heard of the deaths of his noble knights – especially Sir Gaheris and Sir Gareth – he was so overcome with grief that it was some time before he could speak.

'I wish that I had never been crowned!' he said at last, unhappily. 'I have lost the best company of knights that ever served a Christian king. Within the past two days I have lost nearly forty knights as well as the noble fellowship of Sir Lancelot and his family. Alas, that this war ever began!'

Then he instructed the knights around him to say nothing to Sir Gawain of the death of his two brothers. 'For when Gawain hears that Gareth is dead he will go out of his mind. Merciful Jesus, why did Lancelot kill Sir Gaheris and Sir Gareth? Gareth must have loved Lancelot above all other men living.'

'That is true,' said one of the knights, 'but they were killed among many in the turmoil of the battle. Sir Lancelot did not see that they were unarmed and struck them down without knowing who they were. It was an unlucky chance that both were killed.'

'Their deaths will cause the greatest war that has ever been,'
said the king, 'for when Sir Gawain learns that his brother,
Sir Gareth, is dead I shall have no rest from him until I have
destroyed Sir Lancelot and his family. I swear that my heart was
never heavier than it is now. I am sadder at the loss of my good
knights than at the loss of my queen; there are other fair queens,
but never can there be such another fellowship of noble knights.
I am sure that no other Christian king ever held such a
fellowship together. Alas, that Sir Lancelot and I should ever be
at war. Ah, Agravain, Agravain! May your soul be forgiven for
the evil and malice that you and your brother Mordred bore
Sir Lancelot, for it has caused all this sorrow!'

A man then went to Sir Gawain and told him how the queen
had been rescued from the fire by Sir Lancelot, and how twenty-
four knights had been killed in the battle.

'I knew that Sir Lancelot would either rescue her or die in the
field,' said Gawain. 'In truth he would have been dishonoured
had he not rescued her and he has done the right thing by his
knighthood. I would have done the same in his place. But where
are my brothers? I wonder that I have heard nothing of them.'

'I am afraid, sir,' said the man, who had either not heard or not
heeded King Arthur's command, 'your brothers, Sir Gaheris and
Sir Gareth, are dead.'

'No!' cried Gawain. 'I cannot believe that they are dead –
especially not my youngest brother, Gareth.'

'Sir, I fear it is so,' said the man, 'he is dead, more's the pity.'

'Who killed him?' asked Gawain.

'Sir Lancelot killed them both, sir.'

'I cannot believe that he would kill my young brother, Gareth,
for Gareth loved Lancelot above all others – more than he loved
me, his other brothers or even the king. Besides, Lancelot would
have wanted Gareth with him, and I am sure Gareth would have

sided with him against King Arthur and all of us. No, I can never believe that Lancelot killed my brothers.'

'I swear, sir, that it is true; he killed them.'

'Alas!' said Sir Gawain, 'now all my joy is gone!'

He then ran to the king with tears streaming from his eyes. 'Oh, my uncle, King Arthur! My brother Gareth, is slain, and so is my brother, Gaheris – two most noble knights.'

The king wept with his nephew, Gawain, and when they had recovered a little Gawain said that he would like to see his brother, Gareth. 'You cannot see him,' said Arthur gently, 'for I ordered both he and Sir Gaheris to be buried immediately; I knew that you would be overwhelmed by grief, and the sight of young Sir Gareth would have caused you even greater sorrow.'

'Then, sir,' said Gawain, 'pray tell me how Lancelot killed Gareth, for neither Gareth nor Gaheris bore any arms against him.'

'I can tell you only what was told to me – that Sir Lancelot killed them both in the thick of battle and did not know who they were.'

'My lord king and my uncle,' said Gawain solemnly. 'I hereby promise, by my knighthood, that from this day forth I shall pursue Sir Lancelot until one of us has killed the other. I ask you, my lord, as you have my service and my love, to ask your friends to join you and make ready for war. I swear to God that for revenge of my brother, Gareth, I shall seek Lancelot throughout seven kingdoms and I shall kill him unless he kills me first.'

'You don't need to seek him so far,' Arthur replied, 'for I hear that he awaits us all in the castle of Joyous Gard. I also hear that many lords and knights have joined him there.'

'I can believe it,' said Gawain. 'So, my lord, call on as many of your friends as you can and I will call on mine.'

'It shall be done,' said the king, 'and I trust I shall be strong enough to drive him out of the largest tower in his castle.'

King Arthur sent throughout England to summon together all those who would serve him, and assembled a large army of dukes, earls and knights. He told them how Lancelot had taken his queen, then he and his army made ready to lay siege to the castle of Joyous Gard.

Sir Lancelot heard of this and assembled his own army of good knights, for many knights had now joined him at the castle – some for his sake and some for the sake of the queen. Both sides were well equipped for war, but King Arthur's army was so great that Lancelot's men would not meet them in the field. Lancelot, in any case, was unwilling to do battle with the king, and fortified himself in his castle stronghold instead. He had provisions of all kinds, and as many noblemen as he could provide food for within the town and the castle.

King Arthur arrived with Sir Gawain and his mighty army and laid siege to Joyous Gard, both the town and the castle. War was now declared, but Lancelot would not ride out of the castle or allow any of his knights to leave the castle or the town until fifteen weeks had passed. Then, on a day in harvest time, Sir Lancelot looked over the walls of Joyous Gard and spoke in a loud voice to King Arthur and Sir Gawain.

'My lords, you know full well that this siege is useless. Here you will win no honour, but only ill-will and disgrace. If I should choose to come out with my knights I should very soon make an end of this war.'

'Come out, if you dare,' replied the king, 'and I promise I shall meet you in the middle of this field.'

'God defend me!' said Sir Lancelot, 'that ever I should meet in battle with the most noble king that made me knight.'

'Shame upon your fair words!' cried King Arthur. 'You know that I am now your mortal enemy and shall be so to my dying day. You have killed my knights and noble men of my blood that I can never replace. Also, you have slept with my queen for many years and then, like a traitor, taken her away from me by force.'

'My noble lord,' said Lancelot, 'it is true that I have killed your knights and it grieves me to have done so. But should I have allowed them to kill me? I was forced to do battle with them to save my own life. As for my lady, Queen Guinevere, there is no knight living – apart from yourself and Sir Gawain – who dares to prove, by combat with me, that I was a traitor to you. And if you say that I slept with your queen, then I shall make a proper answer to that and prove in battle to any knight in the kingdom that the queen is as true to you as the truest lady living. I admit that it has pleased her to show me more favour than any other knight, and as far as I was able, I have endeavoured to merit her love. There have been many times when, in anger, you have commanded that she should be burnt because of others' accusations. It fell to me to do battle for her, and before ever I parted from her enemy, he always confessed his lie and she was honourably acquitted. At those times, my noble lord, you loved me and thanked me for saving your queen from death, and promised that you would always be my good lord. Now, I think, you reward me unjustly. I would have lost my knightly honour if she had been burnt, especially since, this time, she would have been burnt for my sake. I have fought battles for your queen in other quarters, it is fitting that I should do battle for her in a rightful quarrel for my sake. Therefore, pardon your lady the queen, for she is both good and true.'

'Shame on you, cowardly knight!' cried Sir Gawain. 'My uncle, King Arthur, shall have his queen in spite of you, and kill you both or save you – whichever he chooses.'

'That may well be,' said Sir Lancelot, 'but you know well, Sir Gawain, that if I decided to come out of this castle, you would find winning me and the queen more difficult than the hardest battle you ever fought.'

'Shame on your proud words!' said Sir Gawain. 'As for my lady the queen, I will never dishonour her name. But what cause had you, false and cowardly knight, to kill my brother, Sir Gareth, who loved you more than his own family? You, who made him a knight with your own hands! Why did you kill one who loved you so well?

'Alas, it was my great misfortune that I did not see Sir Gareth or Sir Gaheris.'

'You lie, cowardly knight! You killed them to injure me. And for that, Sir Lancelot, I shall make war upon you and remain your enemy for as long as I live!'

'That, I regret,' said Lancelot. 'But I can see it will be no use to seek a reconciliation with you while are so full of anger. If you were more kindly disposed towards me I am sure I should have the forgiveness of my lord, King Arthur.'

'I do not doubt it, false, cowardly knight,' said Gawain. 'But I shall continue to be ill-disposed towards you and I shall not cease my quest for revenge until I have you at such a disadvantage that you cannot escape me.'

'I trust you in that!' said Lancelot grimly. 'I know that if you do capture me I shall get little mercy.'

King Arthur was prepared to take his queen back and seek a reconciliation with Sir Lancelot, but Sir Gawain resisted this course of action in every way he could, and made many men speak against Sir Lancelot.

When Sir Bors and two other loyal knights, Sir Ector de Maris and Sir Lionel, heard this outcry they called together Sir Palomides, Sir Lavaine, Sir Urry and many other knights. Then all these knights went to speak to Sir Lancelot.

'My lord,' said Sir Bors, as spokesman for them all, 'you know how scornful we are of the insults we have heard Sir Gawain and his followers heap upon you, and we urge you to keep us within these walls no longer. We are fully prepared to ride into the field and do battle with them. My lord, you are acting as a man who is afraid of fighting, and all your fair speeches will bring you no gain, for Sir Gawain will never allow you to be reconciled with King Arthur. Therefore, fight for your life and your right.'

Sir Lancelot shook his head sadly, 'I am most reluctant to ride out of this castle into battle,' he said. Nevertheless, he called to the king, addressing him in a loud voice. 'My lord, King Arthur, since I am urged to ride into battle, I pray that neither you nor Sir Gawain will come into the field.'

'What should we do then?' Gawain called back scornfully. 'Is it not the king's right to fight with you? And it is my right to fight with you, Sir Lancelot, because of the death of my brother, Sir Gareth.'

'Then I am forced into battle,' said Lancelot. 'But I swear to you, my lord Arthur and Sir Gawain, that you will regret it when I do.'

The king and Sir Lancelot then went to get ready for the battle the following morning, and great preparations for war were made on both sides. Sir Gawain chose many knights to lie in wait for Sir Lancelot, so as to set upon him and kill him. And at nine o'clock the following morning, King Arthur was ready in the field with three large armies.

Then Sir Lancelot's fellowship came out of three separate gates in full battle armour. Sir Lionel led the foremost group of warriors, Sir Lancelot came in the middle, and Sir Bors and his knights came out of the third gate. So they rode in good order, as noble knights should, and Sir Lancelot commanded all his men to save King Arthur and Sir Gawain, no matter how.

Sir Gawain rode forward from the king's army and offered to joust, and Sir Lionel accepted the challenge. He was a bold knight and met Sir Gawain fiercely on the field, and there Sir Gawain struck him such a blow that it caused him to fall from his horse as if he had been slain. Then Sir Ector de Maris and various other knights took up Sir Lionel and carried him into the castle.

At once a great battle commenced and many knights were killed, and all the time Lancelot did everything he could to save those in the king's party. Sir Bors and Sir Palomides overthrew many knights, however, for they were fierce and deadly fighters.

King Arthur made several attempts to kill Sir Lancelot, and always Lancelot evaded him and allowed him to continue in the field, refusing to strike back. But Sir Bors engaged with the king, striking him from his horse and then dismounting and drawing his sword. 'Sir, shall I make an end of this war?' he asked Lancelot, for he intended to kill King Arthur.

'No!' Lancelot replied. 'You face your own death if you touch him further! For I will never see the noble king that made me knight either killed or shamed.'

He dismounted quickly from his horse and helped the king to regain his own mount.

'My lord the king,' he said earnestly, 'for the love of God stop this war! You will have no honour unless I do my utmost to oppose you, and I shall always be patient and spare you, even though none of your knights would spare me. I beg you to remember what I have done for you in battles past, for which I am now most unjustly rewarded.'

When King Arthur was again on horseback, he looked at Sir Lancelot and tears sprang to his eyes, for he thought of the noble knight's great courtesy and how he had held him dear above all other knights. And as he rode away from Lancelot he said to himself, 'Alas, alas that this war ever began!'

Both armies then withdrew to rest and to bury their dead, and to examine the wounded men and treat them as best they could. All that night they waited, and the following morning they made ready for battle. On Sir Lancelot's side, Sir Bors led the vanguard (foremost ranks).

Sir Gawain rode forth on the opposing side, as fierce as any boar and with a great spear in his hand. When Sir Bors saw him, he decided to revenge his brother, Sir Lionel, for the injury Sir Gawain had done him. Both knights, knowing each other's strength, fixed their spears and charged with all their might. So fiercely did they meet that each one thrust his spear through the other and both fell to the ground.

At once the battle was taken up by the two armies and there was terrible slaughter on both sides. Sir Lancelot rescued Sir Bors and sent him into the castle, and neither he nor Sir Gawain died of their wounds. Then Sir Lavaine and Sir Urry begged Sir Lancelot to fight at his full strength as they did. 'We see that you are patient with them and spare them, and that does us much harm. Therefore we beg you not to spare your enemies any more than they spare you!'

'Alas, I have no heart to fight against my noble lord, King Arthur,' said Lancelot.

'My lord,' said Sir Palomides, 'no matter how much you spare them, they will show you no gratitude. And if they should ever get you at a disadvantage, you are a dead man.'

Sir Lancelot realised that he spoke the truth and forced himself to fight more fiercely than he had done before, and because his nephew, Sir Bors, was seriously wounded, he exerted himself even further. By sunset, Sir Lancelot's army had the advantage and their horses stood to their fetlocks in the enemies' blood, so many were dead.

Sir Lancelot took pity and allowed King Arthur's men to withdraw, and withdrew his own men into the castle. Both armies buried their dead and put healing ointment on the wounds of the injured. Now that Sir Gawain was among the wounded, King Arthur's warriors were less eager to do battle than they had been formerly.

The war was reported through all the Christian regions and came at last to the attention of the Pope. The Pope considered the great goodness of King Arthur and the high prowess of Sir Lancelot – who was called the greatest knight in the world – and summoned a noble clerk, the Bishop of Rochester. He entrusted the bishop with edicts, sealed with lead, to be taken to the king, commanding him, upon pain of the excommunication of all England, that he take his queen back and seek reconciliation with Sir Lancelot.

The bishop reached Carlisle and showed the king these orders, and when he had read them King Arthur did not know what to do. He would happily have been reconciled with Sir Lancelot, but Sir Gawain would not allow it, although he was willing for the queen to return. So Arthur gave his assurance, in writing, that as he was a truly annointed king he would allow Sir Lancelot to pass in safety, and that the queen would not be reproached by him for anything she had done in the past. He put his royal seal upon this agreement and gave it to the bishop.

The bishop took the written confirmation to Lancelot at Joyous Gard. He explained how he had been sent by the Pope with edicts for King Arthur, and explained the perils involved if Lancelot continued to withhold the queen.

'Sir, it was never my intention to withhold the queen from Arthur,' Lancelot told the bishop. 'I have kept her because she would have been burnt for my sake, and I considered it my duty to save her life and keep her until the danger was past and she could be safely released.'

He then read Arthur's written assurance, and was satisfied. 'I trust Arthur's writing and seal, for he was never untrue to his promise. Therefore, sir, return to the king and recommend me to his Majesty. Tell him that eight days from now, by the grace of God, I shall bring his queen to him myself. And also tell my noble king that I shall speak freely in the queen's defence and that I stand in fear of none but the king himself and my lord Sir Gawain – and that is for the king's sake more than for Sir Gawain's.'

The bishop repeated Sir Lancelot's words to King Arthur, who wept when he heard them. And Lancelot, meanwhile, prepared to return Guinevere to her husband.

Sir Lancelot and the queen rode out arrayed in rich white cloth interwoven with gold. Twelve coursers (large battle horses) followed Sir Lancelot, and upon each was seated a young gentleman clothed in white velvet with a girdle of gold. Each courser was likewise adorned with trappings of white velvet down to the heels, the velvet being splendidly embellished with designs of gold inset with precious stones and pearls.

Then there rode one hundred carefully selected knights, each clothed in green velvet and holding a branch of olive in his hand as a token of peace, and the hundred horses that bore these knights also had trappings of green velvet. Twenty-four gentlewomen – likewise dressed in green velvet and holding olive branches – followed behind the queen.

In this manner Sir Lancelot rode with Guinevere from Joyous Gard to Carlisle. He led his procession throughout Carlisle and into the castle so that all could see them, and many an observer wept at the sight. Then Sir Lancelot dismounted, lifted the queen from her horse and led her to where King Arthur was seated, with Sir Gawain and many great lords before him.

When Lancelot saw the king and Sir Gawain, he took Guinevere gently by the arm and knelt down with her. Many bold knights wept as tenderly as if they had a vision of all their kin dead before them. But the king sat motionless and said nothing. When Lancelot saw his face, he rose to his feet and pulled the queen up beside him.

'My most noble king,' he said, 'by the Pope's commandment and by your own, I have brought my lady, the queen, to you, as justice dictates. And if there is any knight of any rank – except your royal self – who dares to say that she is not guiltless and true to you, then I, Sir Lancelot du Lake, will prove in combat that he speaks falsely. Sir, you have listened to liars and that has caused a great quarrel between us, for the ones who told you these tales were liars, and had it not been for the grace of God they would have killed me. They were armed and prepared beforehand while I was unarmed and unprepared. I was summoned to my lady, your queen, I do not know the reason, but I was barely within the chamber door before Sir Agravain and Sir Mordred arrived and started hurling their false accusations at me.'

'And by my faith, they were right!' said Sir Gawain.

'My lord, Sir Gawain,' said Lancelot, 'in their fighting they proved to be neither the best, nor in the right.'

'Well, well, Sir Lancelot,' said the king, 'I have given you no cause to do to me what you have done, for I have honoured you more than any other knight.'

'My lord,' replied Sir Lancelot, 'if you will permit me to say so, I have done you better service than any other knight. I have often rescued you and Sir Gawain from danger. You both know that I have never met a knight I could not defeat. But I was always glad to meet a good knight who could withstand me on horseback or foot, and such a knight was Sir Carados of the Dolorous Tower. Do you not remember, Sir Gawain, how by superior strength he pulled you from your saddle and bound you crosswise before him to his own saddle-bow? And how I rescued you and killed him in front of your eyes. Do you not remember how I found Sir Tarquin leading your brother, Sir Gaheris, bound and helpless before him, and how I rescued your brother, killed Sir Tarquin and released sixty or more of Arthur's knights from prison? I doubt if I have ever met with knights so strong or skilled as Sir Carados and Sir Tarquin, for they and I fought to the limit. I think, Sir Gawain, that you should remember this, for if I have your good-will I am sure I may have King Arthur's good-will also.'

'The king may do as he pleases,' said Gawain, 'but I swear that you and I shall never be reconciled, for you have killed three of my brothers – and two of them you slew treacherously and without pity, for they bore no arms against you and would never have done so.'

'Would to God that they had been armed!' said Lancelot with feeling. 'For then they may still be alive. As for Gareth, you know full well, Sir Gawain, that I loved him, and as long as I live I shall regret his death, for he was noble, true and courteous. Besides, I made him a knight and he loved me better than any other. As God is my witness, I killed neither Gareth nor Gaheris knowingly; alas, that they were unarmed on that disastrous day!'

Sir Lancelot paused to compose himself, then he lifted his head to address both King Arthur and Sir Gawain. 'This much I can offer you, my lords. I shall start out from Sandwich in the south, and from there I shall go barefoot. After travelling ten miles, I shall have a house built of whatever religion you designate, in memory of Sir Gareth and Sir Gaheris. This I shall do every ten miles from Sandwich to Carlisle, and every house shall be furnished and supplied with all the things a holy place should have. I consider this, my noble king and Sir Gawain, to be fairer and more worthy to their souls than for you to make war against me, for in that you will have no reward.'

All those knights and ladies present wept to hear this. Sir Gawain, however, was unmoved. 'Sir Lancelot,' he said, 'I have heard your fine words and your great offers, but – while the king may do as he chooses – I shall never forgive you for the death of my brothers, especially for the death of my brother, Gareth. And if my uncle, King Arthur, is reconciled with you, he shall lose my service, for you are false to both the king and to me.'

'Sir, there is not a man living who can prove it!' said Lancelot. 'And as you have made such a grave charge against me, Sir Gawain, you must allow me to answer it.'

'No, no,' said Gawain impatiently, 'it is too late for that. The Pope has decreed that my uncle the king shall take back his queen and be reconciled with you, Sir Lancelot, therefore you shall leave as safely as you came, but you shall not remain in this land above fifteen days more. These are my terms, to which the king agreed before you came. Were it not for the Pope's commandment I would fight you with my own hands, and prove that you have been false to the king and to me. And I shall prove it, if ever I find you, once you have left here.'

Sir Lancelot sighed deeply and wept. 'Most noble Christain realm that I have loved above all other realms,' he said. 'In you I have received the greatest part of my honour, and now I must depart in this manner! Truly, I regret that I ever came to this realm to be so shamefully banished, and without cause. But the wheel of fortune is capricious and nothing is constant. Didn't noble Hector of Troy, Alexander the mighty conqueror, and many others fall down on that same shifting wheel? So it is with me. In this realm I had honour, and by me and mine the whole Round Table gained more honour than by any of you. Therefore you must understand, Sir Gawain, that I may live in these lands as well as any other knight. If you, my most noble king, come upon my lands with Sir Gawain to make war against me, I will be as patient with you as I can. But as for you, Sir Gawain, if you come, I pray you do not charge me with treason or felony – for if you do, I must answer you.'

'Do your best,' Sir Gawain replied, 'and hurry away as fast as you can! But mark my words, we shall come after you, and I swear that we shall break down the strongest fort you have.'

'You will not need to do that,' said Sir Lancelot, 'for I will certainly meet you in the field.'

'Make no more speeches,' said Sir Gawain, 'but deliver up the queen and leave this court as quickly as possible.'

'Had I known it would be so, I should have thought twice before coming here,' said Lancelot. 'If the queen was as dear to me as you say she is, I would not have kept her from the fellowship of the best knights under heaven.'

He turned to Guinevere and spoke to her so that the king and all who were with him could hear. 'Madam, now I must depart from you and from this noble fellowship for ever. Pray for me, and I shall pray for you. And if you should be troubled by any false tongues, send word to me immediately. If any knight on earth may deliver you in battle, I shall!'

He kissed the queen, and then addressed the assembled company. 'Now, let us see if anyone here will say that the queen is not true to King Arthur. Let us see who will dare speak.'

No one spoke, and Sir Lancelot led the queen to King Arthur and then departed. The king and all those present wept as Sir Lancelot left the hall, leaving only Sir Gawain dry-eyed and grim. And when he, who had been King Arthur's greatest knight, took his horse to ride out of Carlisle, the people sobbed and wept to see him go.

Lancelot rode back to his castle, Joyous Gard, and from that day forth he called it Dolorous (sorrowful) Gard. Thus the noble Sir Lancelot departed from King Arthur's court for ever.

The Fatal Wound

 any knights were true to Sir Lancelot and declared their allegiance to him, and he bestowed upon them earldoms and dukedoms. He and his family were lords of all France, and with his noble knights, Sir Lancelot sailed from Cardiff to Benwicke (Bayonne) and took possession of his lands there. He crowned Sir Lionel King of France.

Meanwhile, King Arthur and Sir Gawain assembled a great army of sixty thousand warriors and prepared for war against Sir Lancelot. King Arthur made Mordred ruler of all England in his absence, and put Queen Guinevere under his governance; Mordred was Arthur's son and therefore Arthur trusted him with both his land and his queen while he was away.

The king and his great army sailed across the sea from Cardiff and made port on the shores of Sir Lancelot's lands. As they rode to Benwicke, they burnt and destroyed everything in their path.

'Sir Lancelot, it shames us to allow them to ride over our lands in this way!' said Sir Bors, when the news of Arthur's destruction reached Lancelot and his knights. 'You must realise that, no matter how long you allow them to waste your lands, they will do you no favour in return – indeed, they may well capture you!'

Sir Lionel then addressed Sir Lancelot, and he was both cautious and wise. 'My lord,' he said, 'I will give you this advice: let us hold our strong-walled towns until King Arthur's men are hungry and cold, then let us set upon them promptly and cut them down like sheep in a fold, so that ever afterwards foreigners may be warned not to invade our lands.'

Many other noble knights also addressed Sir Lancelot, begging him to retaliate and not to remain passive. 'Sir, there are knights here of royal blood who will not cower within these walls!' they declared. 'Therefore give us leave to do battle as noble knights should, and we will deal with them so that they will curse the day they ever came to this country!'

'My lords,' said Sir Lancelot, 'you well know that I am reluctant to ride out with my knights to shed Christian blood. However, we will keep within our strong walls for now, and I shall send a treaty to Arthur by messenger. Hopefully he will agree that it is better to be at peace than always at war.'

So a lady was dispatched, accompanied by a dwarf, requiring King Arthur to cease his war upon Sir Lancelot's lands. The lady rode on a palfrey (small horse) and the dwarf ran by her side. When she came to King Arthur's pavilion, she dismounted and was greeted by a gentle knight called Sir Lucan, who was the butler. ''Fair lady,' he said, 'have you been sent by Sir Lancelot?'

'Yes, sir,' she replied, 'and I have come to speak with King Arthur.'

'Alas,' said Sir Lucan, 'Arthur would be reconciled with Sir Lancelot, but Sir Gawain prevents him. I pray to God, lady, that you may succeed where others have failed, for all of us who are close to the king know that Sir Lancelot is the best knight who ever lived.'

Sir Lucan then took the lady to where King Arthur was seated with Sir Gawain. And when she told her tale, and told of Sir Lancelot's requirements, King Arthur was moved to tears and all his lords eagerly advised him to be reconciled with Sir Lancelot; all except one, and that was Sir Gawain who still bore

Lancelot great ill-will. 'My uncle,' he said to the king, 'what will you do? Will you turn back now that you have come this far? If you do, the whole world will speak ill of you.'

'You know, Sir Gawain, that I will do as you advise me,' said the king. 'Yet it seems to me that Lancelot's offer is fair and should not be refused. Since we have come so far on this journey I will let you give the lady her answer, for I fear that my own reply would be prompted by pity.'

'Tell Sir Lancelot that it is useless to appeal to my uncle,' Sir Gawain said to the lady. 'If he wanted to labour for peace he should have done so sooner, for now it is too late. And tell him that I, Sir Gawain, swear that I shall pursue him until one of us kills the other.'

At this the lady wept. Then Sir Lucan comforted her, led her to her palfrey, and she mounted and departed for Benwicke with the dwarf. Sir Lancelot was among his knights when she arrived, and on hearing her answer he, too, wept.

'Sir Lancelot, why do you weep?' asked one of the knights. 'Think who you are and what manner of men we are, and let us match your enemies in the field.'

'That may be easily done,' Lancelot replied, 'but I have never been so reluctant to do battle. If you love me, I beg you to be ruled by me in this, for I shall always flee from that king who made me knight, and when I can flee no further only then shall I defend myself. That will be more honourable for me – and for all of us – than to fight with the noble king whom we have all served.'

None of the knights said anything more, and that night they rested. But the following morning at dawn, they looked out to find the city of Benwicke surrounded by Arthur's soldiers, and the besieging army beginning to set up ladders against the walls. Lancelot's men were quick to defend the town, successfully keeping the attackers out and beating them down from the walls. Then Sir Gawain rode up to the main gate in full armour and with a spear in his hand. 'Where are you, Sir Lancelot?' he called. 'Is there not one of your proud knights who will break a spear with me?'

Sir Bors armed himself and rode out of the town to meet the challenge. Sir Gawain charged at him and struck him from his horse, almost killing him. Sir Bors was rescued and carried back into the town and his brother, Sir Lionel, then rode out to revenge him. By good fortune or great skill – and perhaps both – Sir Gawain struck him down as well, and wounded him badly. So Sir Lionel was also rescued and carried back into the town.

Sir Gawain came to the gate every day, and never failed to strike down one knight or another. After this had continued for some time, he rode up to the gate one morning on a noble battle horse, carrying a great spear in his hand. 'Sir Lancelot!' he called loudly. 'Where are you now, false traitor? Why do you hide in holes and crevices like a coward? Come out, traitor knight! I shall revenge the deaths of my three brothers on your body!'

Sir Lancelot's knights and his family drew about him, telling him that now he must defend himself like a knight, or be shamed for ever. 'God help me!' said Sir Lancelot. 'I am saddened by Sir Gawain's words, for now he lays a heavy burden on me. I know that I must defend myself or be called a coward.'

He ordered his strongest horse and his full armour to be brought to the gate tower. Then he called loudly to King Arthur. 'My lord and noble king who made me knight, you know already how sorry I am that you pursue me, and always I have shown you forbearance. Had I been revengeful I would have met you in the field and made your fiercest knights tame. But now I must defend myself, for I can no longer allow Sir Gawain to accuse me of treason. It is greatly against my will that I fight any of your family, but I am driven to it as a beast at bay.'

'If you dare to fight,' shouted Sir Gawain, 'leave your babbling and come on!'

Sir Lancelot armed himself, mounted his horse and rode out to meet Sir Gawain. The two knights faced each other, each with a mighty spear in his hand. King Arthur's men stood apart to

watch, and Sir Lancelot's noble knights came from the city in
great numbers to see their lord do battle. When King Arthur saw
how many of them there were he marvelled and said to himself,
'Alas that Sir Lancelot and I should be opposed, for now I realise
that he has shown me great clemency.'

An agreement was made between the two knights that none
should come to their aid until one of them was killed, or had
yielded to the other. They each turned their horses and rode
some distance apart, then reined about swiftly and galloped
towards each other with all the speed they could muster. Each
struck the other in the centre of his shield and so powerful were
the knights and so massive their spears, that their horses were
unable to withstand the impact and fell to the ground.
Sir Lancelot and Sir Gawain dismounted and stepped aside
from their fallen horses. With their shields in position they
advanced upon each other and fought hand to hand. Their
sword strokes were swift and skilful, and soon the blood was
flowing freely from their wounds.

Lancelot was unaware that Gawain had been given a particular
power by a holy man. Each day, for three hours before noon,
Gawain's might increased to three times that of his normal
strength. As they fought, Lancelot became aware of his
opponent's power increasing in this extraordinary way, and felt
that he was fighting an unearthly fiend rather than a mortal
man. He dodged expertly and covered himself with his shield,
but Sir Gawain gave him so many sharp blows that the onlookers
were amazed that he remained on his feet. Yet only one man
knew what Sir Lancelot was really enduring, for King Arthur
alone knew of his nephew's supernatural gift.

When it was past noon, Sir Gawain's exceptional powers left him
and he had only his own strength. Sir Lancelot felt his enemy's
strength diminishing and stepped close to him. 'Now,
Sir Gawain, I feel you have done your worst!' he said. 'And I
must do my part, for I have suffered many painful wounds from
you today.'

He then gave Sir Gawain such a resounding blow upon his helmet that he fell down sideways, whereupon Sir Lancelot stepped back from him.

'Why do you withdraw?' asked Sir Gawain. 'Turn again, false knight, and kill me outright! For if you leave me now, as soon as I am recovered I shall fight with you again.'

'Then, by God's grace, I shall survive,' said Sir Lancelot. 'But you know that I would never strike a fallen knight.'

So Sir Lancelot left him and returned to his city, and Sir Gawain was taken into Arthur's pavilion, where the best physicians were brought to him to tend his wounds. Sir Lancelot then addressed King Arthur from the city wall. 'Now take your leave, my lord and king,' he said. 'You know that you will gain no honour at these walls, and if I bring my knights out to do battle, many an honourable man will die. Therefore remember old kindnesses and be guided by your conscience.'

'I deeply regret that this unfortunate war ever began!' said the king. 'Sir Lancelot has dealt with me mercifully on every occasion, and shown similar mercy to my kinsmen – as we saw today by the courtesy he showed my nephew, Sir Gawain.'

King Arthur was worried about his nephew's wounds. His army continued to lay siege to the city, but there was now little fighting. Sir Gawain lay sick and broken in his tent for three weeks, receiving the finest medical care that could be obtained. As soon as he was able to ride again, he armed himself completely, mounted a sturdy battle horse and took a huge spear in his hand. Then he rode up to the main gate of Benwicke city and called loudly to Sir Lancelot. 'Where are you, Sir Lancelot? Come out, you false knight and coward! It is I, Sir Gawain, and I will prove with my sword that what I say is true!'

'Sir Gawain, I am sorry that you will not cease your evil words,' Sir Lancelot called back. 'But I know your strength, and you will not do me much harm.'

'Come down, traitor knight!' cried Gawain angrily, 'and make your own words good with your hands! It was my misfortune to be wounded by you, but now I have come to make amends and lay you as low as you laid me.'

'God help me if I was ever so much in your power as you were in mine!' said Lancelot fervently, 'for then my days would certainly be over. Well, since you accuse me of treason in such an unknightly fashion, you shall have your hands full of me!'

Sir Lancelot armed himself, mounted his horse, and rode out at the gate, bearing a spear in his hand that matched Sir Gawain's for size. Both armies were assembled, but both had orders to stand still and watch the battle between the two knights.

Sir Lancelot and Sir Gawain charged at each other and came together with a noise like thunder. Gawain's great spear broke in his hand, his horse's hooves flailed the air, and both horse and man fell to the ground. But Sir Gawain quickly sprang to his feet, holding his shield before him and eagerly drawing his sword. 'Dismount, traitor knight!' he cried. 'My horse may have failed me, but I will not fail you!'

Sir Lancelot dismounted, held his shield before him and drew his sword. The two knights came together and exchanged so many vicious strokes that those who watched were amazed. Then Lancelot felt Gawain's strength dramatically increase, and so he held back and kept under cover of his shield, dodging here and there to avoid the other man's sword and causing him to waste his superhuman vigour. Sir Gawain exerted all his strength and power in trying to destroy his opponent, for as his strength increased, so did his anger and malice. For three hours he inflicted great pain and injury upon Sir Lancelot, who was hard put to defend himself. But at the end of the three hours Gawain returned to his natural strength.

'Sir,' said Lancelot, 'I have twice proved you to be a formidable knight and a man of exceptional power. You have done wonderful deeds in the mornings, through your increased strength, but now I must take my turn!' Sir Lancelot strode up to his adversary and struck such a blow to his helmet, upon his old wound, that Gawain sank down in a faint.

When he recovered, even as he lay on the ground he thrust his sword at Sir Lancelot. 'Traitor knight,' he gasped, 'you can see I am not yet dead, therefore come nearer and finish this battle.'

'I will do no more than I have done,' Lancelot replied. 'I will fight with you when you are standing on your feet. But to strike a wounded man who cannot stand – I will not sink so low!'

He turned away towards the city, and Sir Gawain called after him. 'Traitor knight! When I am well, Sir Lancelot, I shall do battle with you again, for I shall never leave until one of us is dead!'

The siege continued, and Sir Gawain lay sick for nearly a month. Then news was brought to King Arthur from England that ended the war in France and took the king and his army back to his own shores. Sir Mordred, left to rule England in Arthur's absence, had forged letters to say that the king was killed in battle with Sir Lancelot. He had then formed his own parliament and forced his lords to elect him as the new king of England.

Mordred had gone to Winchester, taking Guinevere with him and declaring that he would marry her. He ordered a great feast to be prepared and fixed a day for the wedding. Deeply sad, but aware of her position, Guinevere deemed it wisest to bow to Mordred's will and agree to the marriage. She then asked his leave to visit London to buy the various things a bride needs and, trusting her because of her compliance, Mordred allowed her to go. Once there, she took possession of the Tower of London, quickly provisioned it with food, garrisoned it with loyal men and barricaded herself inside.

When Mordred realised he had been tricked his anger knew no bounds. He took his men to London and laid siege to the tower, making many assaults upon it with guns and engines of war. But the Tower of London proved impregnable, and he had no success.

The Bishop of Canterbury then visited Sir Mordred and remonstrated with him. 'Sir, what are you doing? Will you displease God and bring shame upon yourself and all knighthood? King Arthur is your uncle, being half-brother to your mother, and by that same lady he is also your father. Therefore, how can you wed your own father's wife? I pray you, sir, abandon this idea or I shall be forced to curse you with book, bell and candle (a ceremony of excommunication, **see** 'Viewed from the Wings' p205).

'Do your worst!' said Mordred. 'But I shall defy you.'

'Then I shall not hesitate to do what I have to do,' the bishop replied. 'For you have also told the people that King Arthur is dead, and that is not so.'

'Be silent, false priest!' cried Mordred. 'If you continue to anger me I shall strike off your head!'

So the bishop departed and carried out the cursing with great determination. Mordred looked for him in order to kill him but the bishop fled to Glastonbury where he lived as a hermit priest in a chapel, knowing full well that a terrible war was at hand.

Mordred tried to coax Guinevere from the tower by sending letters and messengers and using fair means and foul. She was not tempted, however, and answered only that she would rather kill herself than marry him. Then he received word that Arthur was returning from France with his great army.

Mordred called the barons to him. The people of England were fickle and ready for change. They were easily persuaded that life with King Arthur had been nothing but war and strife, while with Sir Mordred it was all happiness and peace. So the noble king was defamed, and many of those he had assisted and to whom he had given lands, now had not a good word to say for him.

Mordred rode with a large army to Dover, where it was said that the king would make port. When King Arthur's ships arrived, Mordred was waiting to prevent his father from landing upon the

shores of his own kingdom. There followed a deadly battle by
land and sea, but King Arthur was courageous, and there was
not a knight who could prevent him from disembarking. So he
and his army landed at Dover despite Sir Mordred's powerful
resistance, and they succeeded in driving Mordred back so that
he fled with his army.

When this battle was over, King Arthur had his men search for
those who were wounded or dead. It was then that Sir Gawain
was found in a large boat, so badly wounded that he was more
dead than alive. The king was deeply grieved and took him,
barely conscious, into his arms. 'Alas, Sir Gawain, my sister's
son,' he said, when Gawain stirred and came to his senses, 'here
you lie, the man I love most in the world, and my joy is quite
gone. I confess to you, my nephew, that in you and Sir Lancelot I
had my greatest happiness and trust. Now I have lost you both!'

'Ah, my uncle,' said Sir Gawain, 'you can see that I am close to
death. I have brought it about by my own rashness, for during
this morning's battle I was struck upon the wound that
Sir Lancelot gave me, and now I shall be dead by noon. It is
through my pride that you have all this shame and sorrow. If the
noble Sir Lancelot had been with you, as he would have been,
this unfortunate war would never have started. All your enemies
feared him and were constrained by his presence. But, alas, I
refused to be reconciled with him! Therefore, my good uncle, let
me have paper, pen and ink so that I may write to him myself.'

Pen, paper and ink were duly brought to the dying knight, and
King Arthur gently lifted him into a sitting position so that he
could write his letter.

'To you, Sir Lancelot, flower of all noble knights,' wrote
Sir Gawain. 'I, Sir Gawain, son to King Lot and the noble
King Arthur's sister, send you greeting. On this, the tenth day of
May, I have been struck upon the old wound you gave me at
Benwicke, and through that wound I am brought to my death
bed. I wish it to be known to all the world that I, Sir Gawain,
knight of the Round Table, brought my death upon myself and
there is no blame for it in your actions. I beg you, Sir Lancelot,
come back to England and see my tomb; make some prayer,

whether long or short, for my soul. Also, Sir Lancelot, for the love that was once between us, come quickly and bring your knights, so that you may rescue the noble king who made you knight. He is hard pressed by that false traitor, my half-brother, Mordred, who has crowned himself king and would have married Queen Guinevere if she had not fortified herself in the Tower of London. So, on this tenth day of May, we landed at Dover and the king put Sir Mordred to flight. This letter is written some two hours before my death, and it is written by my own hand and endorsed with my own life blood. Therefore I ask you, most famous knight in the world, to visit my tomb.'

Exhausted with the effort of finishing his letter, Sir Gawain fell into a faint and King Arthur wept for him. When his nephew awoke, the king sent for the priest to give him his last sacrament, and then – very weakly, for there was little life left in him now – Sir Gawain begged his uncle to send for Sir Lancelot and to cherish him above all other knights.

Exactly at noon, Sir Gawain died, and the king gave orders for him to be buried in Dover Castle. Then messengers came to King Arthur with the news that Mordred had taken up a new battle position on Baren-down (Barham Down). The following morning the king and his army rode to meet him, and a mighty battle ensued with many knights killed on both sides. Finally, King Arthur's army gained the advantage and Mordred and his men fled to Canterbury.

The king had the downs searched for those knights of his who were killed. He gave them a Christian burial and treated the wounds of the injured. The people, ever fickle, turned yet again, so that more now supported King Arthur and declared Mordred's war upon the king to be wrong. The king and Mordred agreed that they would meet in battle on the Monday following Trinity Sunday, the battlefield chosen was a down near Salisbury, not far from the sea.

Sir Mordred was able to raise many people in the vicinity of London, the populations of Kent, Sussex, Surrey, Essex, Suffolk and Norfolk remaining, for the most part, loyal to him. Those who had loved Sir Lancelot turned to Mordred and not to the king, because of Arthur's quarrel with Lancelot.

On the night of Trinity Sunday, King Arthur had a strange dream. He saw a platform with a chair upon it and the chair was fastened to a wheel. In his dream, the king sat in this chair wearing the richest cloth of gold, and as he sat there he became aware that, far beneath him, there was water – deep, black and foul – in which all manner of hideous serpents, dragons and wild beasts were swimming. Suddenly, the wheel seemed to turn upside-down so that he fell among these appalling creatures, and each one took him by a limb. The king cried out loudly in his sleep and knights, squires and yeomen came running to awaken him.

The dream had been so horrible that on waking he was bewildered and wondered where he was. He remained awake until it was almost daylight, and then slept lightly and fitfully. As he lay in this half-sleeping state, it seemed to the king that Sir Gawain appeared before him with a number of fair ladies. 'Welcome, my sister's son,' King Arthur said to him in greeting. 'I thought you were dead, but now I see you are alive and I am much beholden to Almighty God. Tell me, dear nephew, who are these ladies who have come here with you?'

'Sir, these are all ladies for whom I fought when I was alive,' replied Sir Gawain, 'and because I did battle for them in righteous quarrels, God has granted their prayers and given them grace to bring me here to you. God has given me leave to warn you of your death; if you fight with Sir Mordred tomorrow morning, as you have agreed, you will be killed, and so will most of those in both armies. Therefore, do not go into battle tomorrow, but secure an agreement for one month from today, so that the fighting shall be delayed until then. Within the month Sir Lancelot will arrive with all his noble knights and rescue you honourably. He will kill Sir Mordred and all who remain loyal to him.'

Then Sir Gawain and the ladies vanished, and the king called his knights and squires and ordered them to bring his noble lords and wise bishops to him. When they arrived he told them of his vision and of how Sir Gawain had warned him that if he fought in the morning he would be killed. Then he commanded Sir Lucan the Butler and his brother, Sir Bedivere the Bold, to make a treaty with Sir Mordred, arranging for the battle to commence one month later. 'Do not be sparing,' King Arthur told them. 'Offer Sir Mordred as much land and property as you think reasonable.'

King Arthur's noble messengers departed and came to where Sir Mordred waited with a formidable army of one hundred thousand men. There they negotiated with him for a long time, and he finally agreed to accept Cornwall and Kent during Arthur's lifetime, and all England upon the king's death. Then they arranged that King Arthur and Sir Mordred should meet peaceably between their two armies to confirm this agreement, and that each should bring fourteen lords with them. When they returned to the king with this news, he breathed a sigh of relief and said he was glad it was done.

When it was time for him to meet Mordred on the field, Arthur warned his warriors. 'If you see a sword drawn, make sure you attack at once and kill that traitor, Sir Mordred, for I do not trust him.'

In similar fashion, Sir Mordred warned his own army. 'If you see any manner of sword drawn, come straight to the attack, for I do not fully trust this agreement and I know that my father seeks revenge.'

So they met according to the arrangement and agreed upon the terms of the treaty. They drank together, without conflict, until an adder crawled out from under a small bush and bit the foot of a knight. When the knight felt this and looked down to see an adder, he unthinkingly drew his sword to kill it. As soon as the two opposing armies saw this sword drawn they immediately arranged themselves against each other in battle formation.

'Alas, this unfortunate day!' cried King Arthur, and he mounted his horse and rode to his army, and Sir Mordred did the same. There followed the most terrible battle ever seen in any

Christian land. Despite the deadly strokes from every direction, King Arthur rode through his enemy's battle formation many times, and fought with great courage, as a noble king should. Sir Mordred, too, acted with skill and bravery.

All day long they fought without pause, and by the time it was almost night, one hundred thousand men had been killed. King Arthur looked at this slaughter and was furious when he saw how many of his men had been killed. As he looked about him he could see only two of his noble knights left standing, Sir Lucan and his brother, Sir Bedivere, both of whom were badly wounded.

'Jesus have mercy!' cried the king. 'What has become of all my noble knights? Alas, that I should ever see such a terrible day.' Then the king saw Mordred in the gathering dusk, leaning on his sword among a great heap of dead bodies. 'Give me my spear,' Arthur said to Sir Lucan, 'for over there I see the traitor who brought about this misery.'

'Sir, let him be,' said Sir Lucan, 'for he brings misfortune. If you can survive this tragic day you will be well avenged. Remember your dream and Sir Gawain's words to you. God has preserved you today. For His sake stop now, my lord. You have won the field, for there are three of us left alive and Sir Mordred alone survives among his knights.'

'Whatever befalls me,' said the king, 'now that I see him standing alone he shall not escape me, for I shall never again have him at such a disadvantage.'

'Then God speed you!' said Sir Bedivere.

Arthur took his spear in both hands and ran towards Mordred. 'Traitor!' he shouted. 'The hour of your death has come!'

When Mordred saw the king, he rushed at him with his sword drawn, but Arthur struck him under his shield with such a mighty thrust of his spear, that it ran right through Mordred's body. As soon as he felt this death blow, Mordred lunged towards his father with all his strength, right up to the hand guard of the fatal spear. Then, holding his sword in both hands, he gathered together the last of his strength and struck the king on the side of the head. The sword pierced Arthur's helmet and skull. Mordred fell to the ground, dead.

Arthur collapsed and Sir Lucan and Sir Bedivere hurried to lift him up. Between them they gently carried him to a little chapel near the sea. Here the king seemed to find some peace and he came to his senses. At the same time a clamour of voices was heard from the field. 'Sir Lucan,' said the king, 'go and find out who is making that noise in the field.'

Sir Lucan mounted his horse, badly wounded though he was, and rode towards the noise. The moon had risen and by its light he saw that robbers had come into the field to plunder what they could from the dead. Many noble knights were being robbed of brooches and rings, and some who were not quite dead were killed for their armour. Sir Lucan rode back to the king as fast as he could and told him what he had seen. 'It is my advice that we take you to the safety of some town,' he said.

'I think that is wise,' the king agreed, 'but I cannot stand for the pain in my head. Ah, Sir Lancelot, how I have missed you today! Alas, that I was ever against you, for now I face my death just as Sir Gawain warned me in my dream.'

Then Sir Lucan and Sir Bedivere lifted up the king and, as he was being lifted, Arthur swooned. In trying to lift him up again, Sir Lucan's injuries proved too much for him; his guts spilled from his gaping wounds and his heart burst. When the king awoke and saw Sir Lucan's mangled corpse, he was devastated.

'Alas,' he said, 'this to me is the saddest of sights, to see how this noble lord died for my sake. He helped me when he needed help himself and he didn't complain, for his heart was set on saving me. May Jesus now have mercy on his soul!' Sir Bedivere then wept for his brother's death.

'Cease your weeping, gentle knight,' said the king, 'for it will not help me. You know that if I lived, the death of Sir Lucan would grieve me for ever, but now my own death fast approaches.

Therefore, Sir Bedivere, take Excalibur, my sword, to the lake, and when you get there, throw it into the water. Then come back and tell me what you saw.'

'My lord,' said Sir Bedivere, 'I shall do as you command and then return with all speed to report to you.'

Sir Bedivere departed to carry out the king's request, but as he rode to the lake he looked more closely at Excalibur. He saw what a noble and magnificent sword it was, and that the haft (handle) and pommel were made of precious stones. 'No good can come from throwing such a magnificent sword into the lake,' he told himself. 'Why, such a loss will surely bring nothing but harm.'

So he hid Excalibur under a tree and then returned to King Arthur and said he had thrown the sword into the lake as he had been commanded. 'And what did you see there?' asked the king.

'Sir, I saw nothing but the waves stirred by the wind on the water.'

'That is not the truth,' Arthur replied. 'Return quickly to the lake and do as I commanded. Do not spare the sword, but throw it in.'

Sir Bedivere rode back to the lake and lifted Excalibur from its hiding place. But, as he held it in his hand, he thought what a waste it would be to cast away something so splendid. So he hid it once more and returned to the king, assuring him that he had thrown Excalibur into the lake. 'What did you see there?' asked the king.

'Sir, I saw nothing but the lapping of the dark waters and the waves.'

'You are a traitor to me!' Arthur said angrily. 'Now you have betrayed me twice. Who would have thought that one I loved and named as a noble knight would twice betray me for the sake of this sword? Now go again, and quickly; your time-wasting has put what remains of my life in jeopardy, for I am cold. Unless you do as I command I shall kill you with my own hands, for you would see me dead for the sake of my rich sword.'

Chastised and ashamed, Sir Bedivere rode back to Excalibur and quickly took it up in his hand. Then he went to the water's edge, bound the girdle of the sword about the hilt, and threw it as far out into the lake as he could. Immediately, a hand appeared above the water, caught Excalibur, brandished it three times and then vanished with the sword beneath the waves.

Sir Bedivere returned to the king and told him what he had seen. Arthur nodded, satisfied, although his life was ebbing away fast. 'Alas,' he said weakly, 'help me from here, for I fear that I have stayed too long.'

Sir Bedivere took the king upon his back and carried him to the edge of the water where a small barge was floating. Within this barge were many fair ladies and among them three queens. They all wore black hoods and wept aloud when they saw King Arthur. 'Now put me into the barge,' said the king.

Sir Bedivere gently lifted Arthur into the barge, where the three queens received him with great mourning, and Arthur laid his head in the lap of one of them. 'Ah, my dear brother,' said the queen, 'why have you stayed away from me so long? Alas, this wound on your head has been too much in the cold.'

Then they rowed the barge away from the land and Sir Bedivere stood beside the water and watched them go. 'My lord Arthur,' he cried, 'what shall become of me now that you go and leave me alone among my enemies?'

'Take comfort,' replied the king, 'and do as well as you can, for I am unable to help anyone now. I must sail to the vale of Avalon to have my wound healed. If you hear no more of me, pray for my soul!'

The queens and the ladies in the barge kept up their piteous crying as the barge sailed majestically out of sight, and Sir Bedivere himself continued to weep and wail even when he could no longer see it. Then he rode into the forest and kept on riding through the night.

In the morning he came across a clearing in the woods with a chapel and a hermitage. Sir Bedivere went into the chapel, and there he saw a hermit, lying face downward to the earth in deep prayer. Near to him was a newly dug grave. When the hermit raised his head, Sir Bedivere recognised him instantly, for he was the former Bishop of Canterbury who had fled from the wickedness of Mordred. 'Sir,' said Sir Bedivere, 'who is it that you pray for so intently?'

'My son,' said the hermit, 'I do not know and can only guess, but this same night at midnight, a number of ladies came here with a corpse and begged me to bury it. They offered one hundred tapers and gave me a thousand gold coins'

'Alas,' said Sir Bedivere, 'it is my lord, King Arthur, who lies buried in this chapel!' With this realisation, Sir Bedivere fainted. When he came to his senses again he begged the hermit to let him remain and live out his days in fasting and prayer. 'I will never leave here of my own free will,' he said, 'but will spend the rest of my life praying for my lord Arthur.'

'Sir, you are welcome to stay with me,' the hermit replied, 'for I know you better than you think I do. You are Sir Bedivere the Bold, and the noble duke, Sir Lucan, was your brother.'

Sir Bedivere told the hermit all that had happened and remained with him and served him in poverty and prayer.

What really happened to King Arthur is not known, except that he was taken away in a ship with three queens, one of whom was Arthur's sister, Queen Morgan le Fay. These ladies brought him to his grave, and a man was buried by the hermit who was, at one time, the Bishop of Canterbury. But the hermit could by no means swear that the man he buried was, indeed, King Arthur.

It is said by some that Arthur did not die, but that he was carried away to another place and that at the right time he will return.

No one can say how true this is, but many declare that the inscription on his tomb reads:

HIC IACET ARTHURUS REX QUONDAM REXQUE FUTURUS

Which is to say:

'HERE LIES ARTHUR, FORMER AND FUTURE KING.'

Viewed from the Wings – Authors and Sources

Geoffrey of Monmouth

Geoffrey of Monmouth was a twelfth-century Welsh author who wrote in Latin. He was also known as Geoffrey Arthur, presumably because his father's name was Arthur. When witnessing documents, Geoffrey signed himself Galfridus Arturus, which means 'Geoffrey son of Arthur'. However, he called himself Galfridus Monemutensis – Geoffrey of Monmouth – which indicates that he must have had some connection with Monmouth in South Wales, and may have been born there or nearby.

His actual date of birth is unknown but was probably about AD 1100, and he died in 1155. He studied and worked at Oxford for some twenty years, attached to Robert of Gloucester, and he posssibly taught there, as he twice signed himself magister (master). Oxford was then a thriving seat of learning but not yet a university, and it was there that Geoffrey wrote his *Historia Regum Britanniae – The History of the Kings of Britain*.

This work, from which the first story in the present collection is taken, is variously described as 'totally fictitious' (M.D. Kennedy, 1995); material of which 'much, if not most, is unacceptable as history; and yet history keeps peeping through the fiction.' (Lewis Thorpe, 1976); 'disguised under the honourable name of history … the fables about Arthur which he took from the ancient fiction of the Britons and increased out of his own head.' (William of Newburgh, 1198).

Geoffrey himself purports to give an account of the British kings over a period of 1,900 years from Brutus, the great-grandson of Aeneas, to Cadwaller (AD 689), 'and especially of Arthur and the many others who succeeded him'. He states that he drew upon a 'most ancient book in the British tongue' (probably early Welsh) which was given to him at Oxford by Walter the Archdeacon and seen by no one else. He translated it into Latin. Yet there is no proof that such a book ever existed and most scholastic evidence is against it, the assumption being that we are a long way from real history.

It seems that Geoffrey of Monmouth drew upon such sources as the historian and scholar, Bede ('The Venerable Bede', 673-735) and Nennius, a Welsh writer living in the ninth century who put together the Latin work *Historia Britonum*. This latter work gives the (supposedly) historical account of King Arthur, and enumerates his twelve battles against the Saxons. Geoffrey's strongest source, however, was probably his own fertile and brilliant imagination! In his time and well into the sixteenth century (with the exception of such sceptics as William of Newburgh), the *Historia Regum Britanniae* was generally accepted as authentic, not only in England, but throughout the continent – especially after Wace, a contemporary of Geoffrey's, had translated it into French. France was a leader in courtly literature in those days, and largely responsible for spreading the Arthurian legend to other parts of the world.

Geoffrey of Monmouth used the title *Prophetiae Merlini* for his book of prophecies (*The Prophecies of Merlin*, Act One), and the name is usually adopted by later writers. Originally, he intended to write the prophecies after the *Historia* was completed, but he was persuaded to publish them first and they probably appeared sometime before 1135. They were dedicated to Bishop Alexander, one of his associates.

The prophecies fall into three separate parts. In the first, Geoffrey is recounting events that occurred – or were assumed to have occurred – at the time he was writing, but would have been in the future for Merlin. The latest historical reference that can be identified is the sinking of the White Ship in 1120 – 'The

Lion's Cubs (the children of Henry I) shall be transformed into fishes of the sea.'

The second part foretells events that were in the future for Geoffrey as well as for Merlin: some, such as the coining of round halfpennies, had already been discussed, while others may have been foreseen by anyone who followed the events of the time. After that, the predictions become wilder and more fantastic and in the third and final part, the symbolism changes from animals and disturbances of nature, to a portrayal of a sort of astrological nightmare. (Parry and Caldwell discuss this in *Arthurian Literature in the Middle Ages.*)

So why did Geoffrey write his *Historia*? Was it meant to be convincing as a historical record and a form of Welsh patriotism, or was it to impress people of importance with whom he was already associated – or was it the vibrant creation of a gifted, poetic mind? Had he lived today, Geoffrey of Monmouth would probably have been a brilliant writer of drama-documentaries, many of which are as enigmatic in their source and accuracy as his *Historia Regum Britanniae*. And before we scorn the credulity of the people of Geoffrey's time, we should remember that the existence of evil spirits, magicians and dragons was generally accepted then.

Despite our modern sophistication, how many of us have not, at some time, at least partially believed in seemingly impossible occurrences or weird phenomena presented to us as 'dramatised facts'? As the first coherent narrative of King Arthur known today, Geoffrey's *Historia*, is of as much importance now as it was nearly nine hundred years ago.

Malory and Caxton

Sir Thomas Malory was born about three hundred years after Geoffrey of Monmouth and died on 14 March 1471. He was a knight, an adventurer and a soldier, and he was also at one time MP for Warwickshire. By 1443 he had already been charged with an assault on property, and it was alleged that in 1450, together 'with other malefactors', he lay in ambush in the woods of Combe Abbey in order to murder the Duke of Buckingham. He was also accused of rape and of leading extensive cattle raids.

In 1451 he was arrested for the first time and spent most of the last twenty years of his life in prison. It was there that he wrote the collection of works that William Caxton published in one volume in 1485 under the title of *Le Morte D'Arthur*, and which has since become such an important source for English Arthurian fiction.

Caxton was the first English printer and a prominent merchant; he set up a press at Westminster in 1476, from where he printed about one hundred books, many of them his own translations from the French. He used eight fonts of type and in about 1480 he began to use woodcut illustrations. On 31 July 1485 he published the Malory texts, describing them in the preface as 'a book of the noble hystoryes of kynge Arthur and certain of his knyghtes' and inscribing it as 'the noble and joyous book entitled Le Morte Darthur'.

Why Caxton should have chosen to publish the work of an obscure 'knight-prisoner' (as Malory referred to himself) is a mystery, yet the book has become a lasting triumph for its author and continues to capture the imagination of modern readers. One of Malory's main sources was the French Arthurian Prose Cycle – the Vulgate Cycle as it is now known. What he did was to 'reduce into English' (Caxton's phrase) various French romances of the thirteenth century which he called his 'French books'. Apart from this process of reduction, his work did not differ very much from the French models. Strangely, no trace of the once-powerful influence of these French prototypes now remains in French fiction or poetry.

For four and a half centuries, Caxton's edition and the many adaptations he made of it contained the only known text of Malory's work. But in 1934 a more authentic text was discovered at Winchester College by W.F. Oakeshott, and it then became possible to separate Malory's text from Caxton's. In his 'Preface to the Christian Reader', Caxton states that he has divided the volume into twenty-one books and that each book is further divided into chapters – 'every book chapytred as here after shal by Goddes (God's) grace folowe'. However, Eugene Vinaver (*Arthurian Literature in the Middle Ages*) points out that we now know the liberties Caxton took were much greater. Not only did he rephrase much of the text but he also tried to make his readers believe that the volume was one single work.

Malory's only single novel is the final 'Tale of the Death of King Arthur'; for the rest he wrote the stories separately, adding to them in a way that meant altering the entire structure – which by no means made comprehension easier for the reader! This restructure also makes for repetition and inconsistencies.

Like Geoffrey of Monmouth before him – and, indeed, like Shakespeare after him – Malory views events from the perspective of his own time. Just as Shakespeare shows us the Elizabethan court, whether we are in Denmark, Athens or Illyria, so Malory – the knight-prisoner – shows us much of his own fifteenth-century England. Inevitably there are anachronisms: he mentions guns, for instance, and the Bishop of Canterbury threatens Mordred with the curse of 'book, bell and candle'. In fact the greater excommunication ceremony of bell, book and candle – during which a bell was rung, a book closed and a candle extinguished – was not introduced into the Catholic Church until the eighth century, at least two centuries after King Arthur's reign (or assumed reign).

Although now available in modern translations, *Le Morte D'Arthur* – the title still generally given to the lengthy cycle of Arthurian legends that Malory completed in 1470 – is by no means an easy read. Even devout scholars of Malory have reservations; as E.K. Chambers said, 'through much of it we walk perplexedly'. But perplexedly or not, anyone willing to take the walk will find much on the way to reward the effort.

The Mabinogion (Culhwch and Olwen)

During Queen Victoria's reign, Lady Charlotte Guest published a translation of eleven Welsh tales under the title of *The Mabinogion* from the *Llyfr Coch o Hergest* (*Red Book of Hergest*) and other Welsh manuscripts, a task in which she was helped by the best-known Welsh scholars of the time (1839–49). The word 'mabinogion' has been mistakenly interpreted, but is now taken as a modern plural of 'mabinogi', meaning 'youth' or 'early days', and being the story of a hero's youth from birth to early manhood. Strictly speaking, the word applies only to the first four stories which are known as the 'Four Branches': 'Pwyll', 'Branwen', 'Manawydan' and 'Math'. However, the meaning has been broadened to include the other seven stories in the collection, where the hero is no longer young.

Arthur is not mentioned in the 'Four Branches', but he appears prominently in five of the remaining seven tales: 'Culhwch and Olwen', 'The Dream of Rhonabwy', 'The Lady of the Fountain', 'Peredur Son of Efrawg' and 'Gereint Son of Erbin'. All the stories have been preserved in two collections, *The White Book of Rhydderch*, and *The Red Book of Hergest*.

'Culhwch and Olwen' is the earliest Arthurian tale in Welsh and is believed to date from before the twelfth century. There is a complete version of it in *The Red Book of Hergest*, a late fourteenth-century manuscript preserved in the Library of Jesus College, Oxford. (*The White Book* is in the National Library of Wales, Aberystwyth.) 'Culhwch' is one of the most important texts for any student of Arthurian literature because of its early date, its many sources – and its introduction of themes and legends that occur in later tales.

In 'Culhwch and Olwen' and 'The Dream of Rhonabwy' there is no sign of French influence; they are products of early Welsh narrative with the use of folk-tale themes from various Celtic sources. 'The Lady of the Fountain',' Peredur' and 'Gereint', on the other hand, are three romances from French originals.

'Culhwch', like the other stories in *The Mabinogion*, was handed down from one story-teller to the next until eventually written down and preserved. To read 'Culhwch' is to experience the rich Celtic tongue almost audibly; as a twentieth-century translator of the tale said: 'The zest of this unknown story-teller still hits one like a bursting wave' (*Arthurian Literature in the Middle Ages*).

Alfred Lord Tennyson (Gareth and Lynette)

Tennyson was born at Somersby in Lincolnshire on 6 August 1809. He attended Louth Grammar School and in 1827 entered Trinity College Cambridge, where two years later he was elected a member of the 'Apostles' – the undergraduate debating society. The same year he won the Chancellor's Gold Medal with his poem 'Timbuctoo'.

A lifelong interest in Arthurian legends was reflected in one of his earlier poems, *The Lady of Shalott* (1832), although he had not yet started on the *Idylls of the King* when he was made Poet Laureate in 1850. In 1855 or 1856 he began work on the first idyll, which he called 'Vivien' and was later to become 'Merlin and Vivien'. In Malory, Tennyson's main source – although he also studied *The Mabinogion* and other Arthurian literature – Vivien is a lake maiden called Nimue and Merlin is completely infatuated with her; but Tennyson's Vivien is a harlot who attempts to seduce the magician.

There were twelve idylls in all, 'Gareth and Lynette' being one of the last to be written (although it relates to an early adventure of the Knights of the Round Table), and it was published in 1872. The source is to be found in Malory's 'Tale of Sir Gareth of Orkney', in the Seventh Book of *Le Morte D'Arthur*, and Tennyson adapted it respectfully but freely, giving a charming little acknowledgement to Malory at the end:

'And he that told the tale in older times [Malory]
Says that Sir Gareth wedded Lyonors,
But he, that told it later, [Tennyson himself] says Lynette.'
His letters prove that he found the poem particularly hard to compose, although there is no sign of this in the finished work. He would like to have written it in drama format (characters names on the left, followed by dialogue) but did not feel at liberty to do so.

Some critics have accused Tennyson of 'sanitising' the legends to make them more acceptable to his Victorian readers; whether or not this is true, his language and use of allegory and mysticism give them a special beauty. Compare, for example, Culhwch's arrival at Arthur's gate in *The Mabinogion*, to Tennyson's description of the same gate as first seen by Gareth and his companions. Culhwch is greeted by Arthur's chief porter, who appears to us in decidedly humorous vein, while Tennyson, on the other hand, has Gareth and his two companions arrive at a Camelot shrouded in mist and mystery.

The sequence of the twelve *Idylls of the King* as it is now printed did not appear until 1891. Tennyson died at Aldworth on 6 October 1892.

Arthurian Influence on Modern Culture

Questing and jousting were two important activities for the knights of the Round Table, particularly after Arthur had defeated the Saxons. A quest would frequently lead to a joust but it could happen the other way about – and often did. If a knight was killed or seriously wounded in a joust then one of his relatives, or his lady, would seek retribution. If the relative happened to be another knight he would undertake the task himself, but a lady would seek revenge as a boon (gift) from a knight. If she was a lady of high birth, she would go to the king himself, who would designate a knight to perform the quest for her.

Knights who were jousting at tournaments would usually wear a lady's favour in the form of her scarf or a colourful ribbon which they would tie to their helmets. But questing also included the hunting and slaying of giants, dragons and beasts, as in the case of King Pellinore and the Questing Beast, for example (although his quest was singularly unsuccessful, as he never caught it).

The spread of Arthurian literature meant that mimicry of Arthurian pageantry and jousting became very popular world-wide in the thirteenth, fourteenth and fifteenth centuries. The first evidence of such re-enactments comes from Cyprus in 1223, when the lord of Beirut celebrated the knighting of his eldest sons. In 1446, King René of Anjou in France went to great lengths to represent accurately the jousts held by Arthur's knights. He had a wooden castle constructed, which he called 'Joyeuse Garde', a beautiful lady leading the king's horse, a dwarf dressed as a Turk bearing the shield, and animals from the royal menagerie including lions, tigers and even unicorns – or so it was said.

Today there are occasionally imitative medieval jousts held in castle grounds or at more ambitious outdoor fêtes, but by far the most popular quest participation sport is to be found in computer games or role-playing activities.

You only have to read the copy that goes with some of the best-known computer games to see the influence of Arthurian tradition: 'the game sets the players on a nightmarish, knife-edge quest to destroy the evil rulers who once controlled them,' or a 'quest to banish the Shapeshifter Witch and free the good wizard…' and so on.

Role-playing games are probably the most realistic imitations of Arthurian legends. Considerable research goes into most of them, as is evident from the books and magazines that set out some of the story-lines. In a recently published role-playing game, one section is entitled 'The Dolorous Blow' and contains obviously Arthurian-based instructions. This particular game has an interesting slant, because the Saxons are the heroes and Arthur's troops are the villians!

The media constantly reflects the lasting popularity of the legends. The mythology is even apparent in Western films, where battles against lawlessness predominate and the cowboy hero represents the chivalrous knight. The first Western to be made was *The Great Train Robbery* in 1903, followed later by such classics as *Stagecoach* and *High Noon*.

The musical, *Camelot*, based on T.H. White's delightful novel *The Once and Future King* (the title comes from Malory's epitaph to Arthur: REX QUONDAM, REXQUE FUTURUS) had great success in America – despite one critic's remark that 'the audience comes out of the theatre humming the scenery' – and was very well received when it opened in London at Drury Lane on 19 August 1964, directed and choreographed by Robert Helpmann. It was launched again for the Covent Garden Festival in June 1996, but sadly, sank without trace – apart from an unfavourable comparison to *My Fair Lady* and caustic comments about 'lusty knights and leap-frogging maidens'. But Arthur can hardly be blamed for that!

Bibliography

ASHE, Geoffrey
King Arthur: the Dream of a Golden Age (Thames and Hudson, London, 1990)
The Landscape of King Arthur (Webb and Bower, 1987)
King Arthur's Avalon (Fontana Paperback, 1973)
Mythology of the British Isles (Methuen, London, reprinted 1996)

BARBER, Richard
King Arthur, Hero and Legend (The Boydell Press, Suffolk, reprinted 1986)

BENHAM, Patrick
The Avalonians (Gothic Image Publications, Glastonbury, 1993)

GEOFFREY of MONMOUTH
History of the Kings of Britain, translated by Lewis Thorpe (Penguin Books, 1966)

JONES, Gwyn and Thomas
*Trans. *The Mabinogion* (Everyman's Library, Dent, London, reprinted 1986)

LANCELYN GREEN, Roger
King Arthur and his Knights of the Round Table (Puffin Books, 1953)

LOOMIS, Roger Sherman
Ed. *Arthurian Literature in the Middle Ages* (Oxford University Press, 1959)

BIBLIOGRAPHY

MALORY, Sir Thomas
Morte D'Arthur (The Walter Scott Publishing Company, London, undated)
King Arthur and His Knights, selected tales edited by Eugene Vinaver (Oxford University Press, 1975)

MORRIS, John
**The Age of Arthur – a history of the British Isles from 350 to 650* (Weidenfeld and Nicolson, London, reprinted 1989)

TENNYSON, Lord Alfred
**Idylls of the King* edited by J.M. Gray (Penguin Books, 1996)

WESTWOOD, Jennifer Albion
**A Guide to Legendary Britain* (HarperCollins, reprinted in paperback 1994)

WHITE, Terence Hanbury
**The Once and Future King* (HarperCollins, reissued in Fontana 1987)

*Most of the books that are out of print may be borrowed from a public library.

Index